woman overboard

woman overboard

how passion saved my life

jo kadlecek

FRESH AIR BOOKS®

Nashville

Cover design: The DesignWorks Group/www.thedesignworksgroup.com
Interior Layout: Nancy Terzian/www.buckinghorsedesign.com
First printing: 2009

Library of Congress Cataloging-in-Publication Data
Kadlecek, Jo.
  Woman overboard : how passion saved my life / Jo Kadlecek.
    p. cm.
ISBN 978-1-935205-06-7
1. Kadlecek, Jo. 2. Christian biography. I. Title.
BR1725.K33A3   2009
277.3'083092—dc22   2009014001

Printed in the United States of America

FOR CHRIS,
the most passionate person I know

c o n t e n t s

The opposite of love is not hate, it's indifference.
The opposite of art is not ugliness, it's indifference.
The opposite of faith is not heresy, it's indifference.
And the opposite of life is not death, it's indifference.
—Elie Wiesel

PROLOGUE

Longing for Passion

Compared to my heart's desire
the sea is a drop.
—Adélia Prado, *The Alphabet in the Park*

For most of my life, I have had a strange fear of water . . .

I am floating on my back in the sea, drifting slowly away from
a sandy summer morning. A June sun warms my cheeks. Shoulders
relaxed, arms out, toes just inches above the water, I am rocked
back and forth by soft waves. I look up to absorb the sky's color: it
is pale compared to the deep ocean blue that carries me further into
the moment.

I float still on my back, now in the middle of a mass of Atlantic.
Or Pacific, I'm not sure which. Gray clouds swirl above me. Out
here, except for the pound of the waves in my ears, it is noiseless,
lonely, void. I feel the water's huge presence toss me, a piece of
human driftwood.

Head back, palms up, I am on top of the water even as I watch an enormous barge coming toward me. Out of nowhere. The bottom of the ship is as flat as the surface of the ocean and within seconds it overtakes me, dunking me into the deep as it proceeds forward.

Soon I am completely submerged and I look for a place to come up for air. But there is none.

The barge dwarfs the ocean's surface and I cannot see the clouds. But I don't panic. I don't fight. Or punch. Or grope for anything to save me. My heart doesn't beat faster, and my stomach doesn't flip over with fear. My hands simply feel the water as if it were a blanket, and I continue to sink. Motionless.

Under the barge. Away from air.

I swallow and the saliva tastes of salt. My eyes sting from staring at the barge above me, which fills the space where the sky once was. Thoughts clog my mind: I will never again feel the sun on my face. Or hear the whispers of the waves. Or touch my husband's hand. I know there is no way out.

I know I have lost.

I shake my head hard. Groggy. Again I force my head left, then right, and finally my eyes open, fixed on a pillow, a lamp, a bedpost. Terror streams into the early-morning room the way shafts of sunlight did in the afternoon. Sweat lines my face, and my hands tremble. My body groans, knowing it's not time to let go of sleep just yet. But when my eyelids drop, the barge is pushing me underwater again, so I force myself awake.

Sleep is supposed to give you life, not steal it.

My husband and I had joined friends at a beachside cottage for a reprieve from New York's crowded life. Yesterday we built sand castles and pyramids, ate peaches that felt as soft as the terry cloth towels we lay on, and laughed at the waves that rolled over our toes.

One friend floated in the sea.

Obviously the image stayed in my head as I went to bed that night.

And the image haunts me even now. Why did I feel so little emotion when the danger of the water was so great? When the barge swept over me and cut off any connection to air, why was I passive, resigned, limp? Why did I not fight for my life?

The questions—not the ocean—were the most terrifying aspect of the dream. Not the fear of being lost at sea or the enormous power of the water or even the risk of drowning. No, I had lost my passion. For living.

And there was no greater terror to me than indifference toward being alive.

Nothing is so intolerable . . . as being fully at rest, without a passion, without business, without entertainment, without care.

—Blaise Pascal, *Pensées*

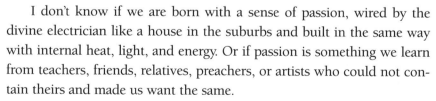

I don't know if we are born with a sense of passion, wired by the divine electrician like a house in the suburbs and built in the same way with internal heat, light, and energy. Or if passion is something we learn from teachers, friends, relatives, preachers, or artists who could not contain theirs and made us want the same.

Maybe it's both.

I only know I don't want to live without it. To be counted among the walking dead, like a character from Jack Finney's *Invasion of the Body*

Snatchers, first published in 1955. The book (not the movie) had a big impact on me. Remember the story? At first, I thought (and you might have too) it was just another silly science-fiction novel. Alien pods come to earth, suck the life out of whatever living creatures allow them access—which, of course, most humans do. Then the pods begin to take on those forms, fingernails and all. But the narrator and protagonist, Dr. Miles Bennell, fights the pods, or tries to. Even as the invaders come to power—one of whom is in the human form of a professor named Budlong—Miles challenges them:

> "There was only one way Wilma Lentz knew Ira wasn't Ira. Just one way to tell, because it was the only difference. There was no emotion, not really, not strong and human, but only the memory and pretense of it, in the thing that looked, talked, and acted like Ira in every other way."
>
> My voice dropped. "And there's none in you, Budlong; you can only remember it. There's no real joy, fear, hope, or excitement in you, not any more. You live in the same kind of grayness as the filthy stuff that formed you."

Miles, of course, surprises the aliens with his tenacity to *live*. And as a result, the pods no longer feel welcome on earth—go figure—and fly back from whence they came.

I still remember putting down that book, and pleading with God, with myself, with anyone who'd listen, "Don't let me be gray!" Though it's tempting to give in or give up, to stay busy or look engaged with the *memory and pretense* of living, we all know that it is not the same.

In fact, that pretense stuff can be scary business. Which is why, I suppose, Finney's story first, and my dream later, were both so disturbing to me. Maybe the dream invaded my sleep at a time when my days at work seemed insignificant, irrelevant even. I felt unnoticed. Maybe it happened because my husband and I had been talking of leaving the only home we'd ever known together to make another in a nearby state, and change can burrow its fearful way into a soul like a tick. Or maybe it was a piece of the world's chaos thrown into my head like a grenade. God knows, the nightmares of death and decay on every corner of our planet these days can scare the daylights out of me.

But to give up the fight to stay alive—to let the pods win—and forgo the possibility of ever again feeling *"real joy, fear, hope, or excitement,"* to *not* care how I'd find my next breath of air, well, the very idea of such complacency evoked terror in me. Not only did it force me from a physical sleep, it shook my soul awake and slapped my sensibilities into noticing the gift of the man beside me, the friends next door, the health in my bones. It made me suddenly thankful for pillows and roofs, for peaches and towels, for feet and waves and soft mushy sand. And it made me ashamed of my pitiful blindness to these gifts.

At least for a little while until I fell asleep again. Still, that dream did make me stare long and hard—it does now as well—in between the daily breaths of routine, at the most intriguing question I've ever heard, the question that drives the stories and thoughts you are about to read in the following pages: *What does it mean to be alive?*

Miles knew.

For those of us who don't exist in novels but in this crazy, transient world, I'm beginning to think the answer and the question are the same thing.

Sometimes those answers and questions come in many forms like a dark dream. Mine bumped me back to this trail I began walking forty-something years ago, one that has taken on the form of wonder or wanderlust, agony or irony, love or loveliness along the way. Each form helped me see that this question of being *alive* demands utter abandon but is somehow as familiar and safe as home.

It replenishes restless souls. Like mine.

People can think correctly and behave rightly and worship politely and still live badly—live anemically, live bored and insipid and trivial lives.
—Eugene Peterson, "The Holy Stump," in *Subversive Spirituality*

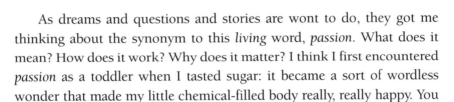

As dreams and questions and stories are wont to do, they got me thinking about the synonym to this *living* word, *passion*. What does it mean? How does it work? Why does it matter? I think I first encountered *passion* as a toddler when I tasted sugar: it became a sort of wordless wonder that made my little chemical-filled body really, really happy. You know the feeling: a surge of excitement rises from your belly, makes your eyes wide, and you laugh and smile and holler all at once. You feel giddy, full, protected. You just can't help yourself.

I suppose the next time I recognized passion, it was the fuel that transformed regular moms and pops into heroes who conquered corporate evils and dirty diapers to teach me how to hit a softball or read a book. They loved the doing of the deed and made me want to love it too. Infected, enabled, equipped. *Saints with day jobs*, as Robert Benson likes to call them.

As an adult, I began to notice passion more as a vision that painted canvases, recited poems, or recounted stories in books and stages and films, making audiences gasp or cry in response. Changed and moved, I confess that the art of passion or the passion of art—I've never been able to figure out which is which—still leaves me marveling and wanting to stare.

At more somber times in my life, I've been reminded how passion has been the song that sustains workers in hot fields or victims in unimaginable terror. It is the relentless will to survive—Miles-like—even when all around you is deep sorrow or agonizing suffering. I have been told that in prison cells, in hospital rooms, and on battlefields, when life's sting can be excruciating but the grip on hope secure, this question of being alive is sung the loudest. A little like the reality that *she who is for-given much, loves much.*

And the older I get, the more I rediscover how passion not only guides but also grows, full of paradoxes, beauty, and truth: meaning erupts from nothing, joy emerges from pain, life-giving water comes from Jesus' sacrificial blood spilled in a week we've come to call Passion. And light bursts from death's darkness. It's this place I'm drawn to, attracted by its many colors and scents, lessons and insights. Here, where I must first be motionless, then aware, and soon, full.

Of course, words change meaning through the centuries just as they do during the seasons of a person's life. *Passion* today does not mean what it did, say, in the third century. In fact, when I've asked modern people— like those I passed last week on 42nd Street in New York—they equated passion with sex, romance with eroticism, and desire with lust. Some on Wall Street or in the Bronx thought of intensity or rage when they heard the word *passion*. CEOs and Hollywood stars have called passion a wild, unyielding drive to snatch success by any means possible. Yet those in the business of caring for souls as well as those in academia said passion was an affection of the mind or a concentrated allegiance to some thing or some one. Priests and preachers countered and exclaimed that its very history began in Gethsemane, moved to a cross, and ended at an empty tomb. *Passion*, they proclaimed, has another name: Holy Week.

Each of the contemporary interpretations seemed linked to this ques-tion of being alive. Yet they also made me all the more curious. So the teacher in me picked up a dictionary (remember those?), flipped to the

Ps, and found these—and more—confirmed in the word's history. From the Medieval Latin word *passio*, *passion's* meaning comes *first* from "the sufferings of Jesus in the period following the Last Supper and including the Crucifixion, as related in the New Testament."

Living passionately, then, somehow takes us to the upper room?

From Late Latin, *passion* is "physical suffering, martyrdom, or sinful desire." From *passus*, the past participle of *pat*, it is simply "to suffer," an option oddly left out in my modern-day survey. As the word evolved in languages and cultures, the word took on a variety of other meanings: "a powerful feeling, such as love, joy, hatred, or anger; strong sexual desire; lust," or "the intense object of such love or desire." *Passion* also meant "boundless enthusiasm, an overwhelming emotion, or an archaic martyrdom that includes a state of acute pain, or an irrational but irresistible motive for a belief or action." Think *fervor, fire, zeal,* and *ardor* as synonyms, and zeal as "a strong, enthusiastic devotion to a cause, ideal, or goal and tireless diligence in its furtherance."

For anyone eager to fight the real-life "pods" that try to suck out our lives, I suspect there is truth and wisdom in all these definitions. Each helps us resist the powers that can pull us toward indifference; each sharpens our vision and fuels our steps as we wander through the earthly matters we call living.

The words become gifts for the road, and for the stories we're given to tell. I know this to be true. For me, and in the chapters that follow, I've discovered, for instance, that passion is born in the *boundless enthusiasm* of adventure and shaped by the *powerful feelings* unlocked in art. It's fed in the sometimes *irrational but irresistible* arenas we call *vocation*. And it grows from the *intense desires* of romance along with the *acute pain* of suffering—and sometimes in my life the two have become one.

Before you turn the page, I must tell you something else. The more birthdays I celebrate the more I keep discovering that the dictionary is right: passion's fullest meaning does seem bound to the Man of all passions, Jesus Christ. Because from that place near the grace of *his* suffering, I am invited into the care of others, to *suffer with* them—in the fellowship of *com*passion. (*Com* means "with" and *passio*, "to suffer.") From this togetherness of compassion, this community of sufferers—our pains somehow feel lighter, our hearts gladdened along the way. I think we're even free to skip along the road because someone has offered us a hand. And these days, in the midst of so much earthly madness, we could use more skipping.

Each of these and all of these meanings together become the question and the answer, the journey and the reason we take another step in the first place. And then another. It's hardly simple or easy, because passion—like you or me—cannot be confined to a category. In fact, it gasps, trembles, and sweats until it is recognized for what it is: a gift that wakes us up again each morning, calling us to another clue to the mystery of being alive.

It did, after all, draw me out of the water.

*Read the directions and directly you will be
directed in the right direction.*
—Doorknob in the film
Alice in Wonderland

ad·ven·ture (ăd-věn´chər) [Middle English
aventure, from Old French, from Latin
adventurus, future participle of advenire,
to arrive; see ADVENT.]

Noun: An undertaking or enterprise of a
hazardous nature.
    An unusual or **exciting** experience: *an
adventure in dining.*

Verb: To venture upon; undertake or try.
    To proceed despite risks.

ONE

Wanderlust

and the adventures I've had to take

The world is a book, and those who do not travel, read only one page.
—Saint Augustine *agree*

There are those who say that if you believe in God, your life will always be comfortable and safe. I have found the opposite is true.

Let me explain.

The first time I was born was quite an adventure.

That July night was darker than most in northern California, the story goes. Rain descended in Niagara proportions on the small Oakland suburb where my mother—round with life—fumbled for the light switch and her husband. Thunder shook their simple three-bedroom house, waking my father in time to see my mother stumbling toward him. He tossed a suitcase in the back of the station wagon, helped his wife into the front seat, and charged out of the driveway like an ambulance driver in enemy territory.

Wipers beat hard against the window, my mom groaning and breathing to the rhythm on the glass. Fog hovered around streetlights, casting strange stripes of light on the road. The rain pounded harder as my dad's foot on the gas pedal felt the tension of the night: hurry slowly, careful danger. When he turned the corner onto Main Avenue and glanced down at his dashboard, he caught a dreadful sight: the car was out of gas. They would not make it to the hospital.

He screeched into the first service station he saw, put the car in park, and jumped out to fill the tank. My mother complained of a full bladder and climbed out of the car, headed toward the restroom. Winds gushed around her. Lightning cracked the sky. Halfway to the ladies' room, her water broke, spilling onto the already drenched pavement. She retreated back to the car and yelled for my father. Within seconds, they were driving over the median onto the busy street, dodging in and out of cars until finally they forced their way into the emergency entrance of Hayward Hospital. A team of nurses and orderlies whisked my mom away and shouted to her nervous, soaked husband that he'd have to stay in the waiting room (it was the 1950s, after all). He obeyed, sweating and pacing under the fluorescent lights, until three hours later a doctor appeared and announced that mother and child were fine.

For years I've clung to the story as mine. I have always reveled in the exciting way I came into the world, the forces my parents encountered just to usher in my safe arrival, the many risks and dangers they faced to help me enter the planet. Oh, the sheer adventure of it all! I have even credited (or blamed, depending on the day) that dramatic entry with godlike powers in shaping who I am today. It is why I wander, I tell friends.

How much the human soul needs a story to believe, one to help her make sense of the journey.

Imagine my crisis of identity, then, when I phoned my dad, asked him to tell me again the story of that harrowing night, and all he did was laugh. I pressed him. Eager for another round of drama and suspense, I recounted the details as I understood them, but since my memory of the night was a bit fuzzy, I asked for specifics. Give it to me line by line, I said to him, because doggone it, I want to boast about the marvelous adventure of my *birth* day to all the world. He laughed. Again.

"Sorry, Kid, that was your brother," he said with no more emotion than if he'd just flipped on the Weather Channel. "The way you were born, well, there wasn't much to it."

What?! How had I confused this family myth all these years by believing it was my own? Why did my brother get all the good stories?

I swallowed a big chunk of air and gave myself a moment to reflect.

I knew the answer: if I were honest, I had claimed the myth as mine because, well, I wanted my birth to matter. I wanted significance. Most of us do, don't we?

And so the second time I was born—in story form and reality—goes like this: northern California was having a typical summer afternoon, sunny, breezy, occasional scattered showers. My very pregnant mother waddled around at her secretarial job in a doctor's office, while my father audited a project in Napa for the accounting firm that employed him. Around 2:00 in the afternoon, his phone rang. My mom was calling to tell him the contractions had started. When he asked if he should drive the two hours back to Hayward, my mom told my dad not to bother. This was no big deal, she said; after all, how hard could baby number three be after two relatively easy births? Besides, she worked for a doctor. Who—after my parents hung up the phone—simply drove my mother to the hospital three miles away, walked her into the delivery room, and helped pull me to earth by dinnertime.

The next morning my father drove to the hospital, kissed my mother on the cheek, held me for a second, and went back to auditing. Five days later my mom and I came home. A year later, when my father was offered a better accounting job, my parents moved my brothers and me to the suburbs of Denver. We lived in a brick house in a neighborhood of identical brick houses with neighbors who looked exactly like we did. It was all quite ordinary.

And for the next nineteen years that is where we stayed.

> *So many people live within unhappy circumstances and yet will not take the initiative to change their situations because they are conditioned to a life of security, conformity, and conservatism, all of which may appear to give one peace of mind, but in reality nothing is more damaging to the adventurous spirit within a man than a secure future.*
>
> —Jon Krakauer, *Into the Wild*

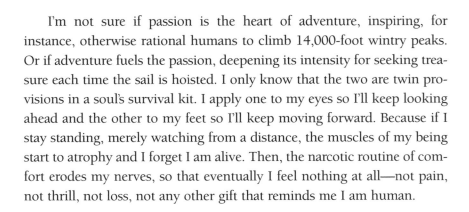

I'm not sure if passion is the heart of adventure, inspiring, for instance, otherwise rational humans to climb 14,000-foot wintry peaks. Or if adventure fuels the passion, deepening its intensity for seeking treasure each time the sail is hoisted. I only know that the two are twin provisions in a soul's survival kit. I apply one to my eyes so I'll keep looking ahead and the other to my feet so I'll keep moving forward. Because if I stay standing, merely watching from a distance, the muscles of my being start to atrophy and I forget I am alive. Then, the narcotic routine of comfort erodes my nerves, so that eventually I feel nothing at all—not pain, not thrill, not loss, not any other gift that reminds me I am human.

In the passion for adventure—or the adventure of passion—there is always something new to stir my blood, some discovery that keeps my heart from shriveling, some hint of the bigger Story to pursue.

Granted, some souls seem better equipped than others to endure a regimen of living. They wake each morning to eggs for breakfast, go to the same job they've had for seventeen years, and come back as the sun sets to the house they left that morning in the same town where they've lived, banked, voted, and had their hair cut for just as long. I admire these people for their stability, ritual, and control, but I do not understand them. Adventure to them seems merely trying a new barber every now and then.

But I admit I have never stayed at the same job for long. Psychologists might diagnose this as symptomatic of a deeper problem. And I would agree: I have always wanted more, needed more. Yes, mine is a restless soul, prone to wander, as the old hymn says, *Lord, I feel it.* Friends tell me they use only pencils when writing my address in their books. Because I'm hungry to go, always craving the new, itching for something . . . else.

yup

Which might be why my ordinary family in our ordinary American suburb made a habit of getting me out of the house. YMCA summer camps in the mountains, attendance at the theater downtown, vacations in the station wagon, softball tournaments out of state, all kept both head and body moving. When I complained of boredom, I was taken to the library (thank God!) or the local athletic club. When I whined about the same old everything in our same old neighborhood, I was driven to the city for professional basketball games or a small town on Colorado's eastern plains for family reunions. Like a baby's appetite, my need for exploration was constant, always wanting more; and my life rarely made sense without it.

I have not outgrown that need.

What I did not realize then, however, was how much this slight affliction of wanderlust required a home. I could travel the world by boat or by book, see the sights of the continent through my eyes or my imagination, but if I didn't have some familiar place to return to, some refuge to replenish me, I would become nothing more than a hopeless nomad. Any sailor knows that adventure is exciting only when you can come home again. Home is your anchor, keeping you from drifting into meaningless waters. And giving you the courage to set sail in the first place.

> *"Well!" thought Alice to herself. "After such a fall as this, I shall think nothing of tumbling down-stairs! How brave they'll all think me at home! Why, I wouldn't say anything about it, even if I fell off the top of the house!" (Which was very likely true.)*
>
> —Lewis Carroll, *Alice's Adventures in Wonderland*

When I was seven years old and my mother was engrossed in her Wednesday afternoon bridge game in our dining room with the neighborhood ladies, I took my first solo trip. I didn't know that morning when I woke up that I would go exploring later, nor did I ask permission. I simply took inventory of my summer circumstances that day—brothers on their bikes somewhere in the neighborhood, Dad at work, Mom glued to her cards—and decided to take advantage of the situation. I walked into my bedroom, picked up my pink ceramic pig, shook it to make sure it had enough pennies to see me through a few days, and strolled past the bridge ladies out the front door.

No one noticed.

I hurried down our street, dodging in and out of parked cars, hiding behind each like I was a soldier in a war zone. Then I'd press my pink bank to my belly and make a run to the next parked station wagon until finally I was around the corner from our brick house and in front of the local swimming pool that doubled as an ice-skating rink in the winter. The club was at the end of the street and sat parallel to the interstate highway government officials had built since we moved here. I had no idea that the highway provided a direct route to the ski resorts in the Rocky Mountains; I only knew it interrupted the virgin field my brothers and I played in before it was built.

Across from the swimming pool, the government had also built a high pedestrian bridge enclosed by chicken wire, that woven metal mesh you can poke your fingers through. The bridge jutted out above Interstate 70—it felt like fifty yards above the road—and dropped into the next suburb by way of another set of cement stairs. I hid behind a trash can for a second to make sure I was safe, glanced at the whirling highway, and darted toward the bridge.

I climbed the steps to the top of the bridge, careful to hang on to my bank with each upward motion. I'd been up here before with my brothers, but this was the first time I'd stood in the center of the bridge by myself. It was the first time I spit on the cars below without anyone else to witness the splattering. Usually my brothers and I shared the excitement of hurling saliva onto the traffic below. But since delinquency is fun only when someone's watching, I tired quickly of the spitting game, remembered my mission, and kept walking.

By the time I jumped off the last step and onto the asphalt on the other side, I spotted my treasure. The Big Top convenience store, a round solitary building with a roof like a circus tent, sat on the corner of the bridge street and the next busy one that paralleled Interstate 70. I ran toward a tree a few yards away, angled next to it to make sure no one could see me—not that anyone was looking—and then bolted toward the next bush to do the same. Within minutes I was in front of the Big Top and strolled in as if this was something I did every day. Then I found the candy section.

I set down my pig in the aisle and scooped Bazooka Joe bubble gum, Tootsie Pops, and pastel-colored candy necklaces into the bottom of my T-shirt that I had stretched out below my stomach to form a bag. I squatted toward the pig and waddled to the cashier, where I dumped all my loot on the counter. I opened the bank and poured out $3.37 in pennies next to the Tootsie Pops. The clerk sighed, counted every coin, and dropped each into the register. Then he swept my sweet treasure into a brown bag and sent me out the door.

Armed with enough food to last a lifetime, I planted myself at the center of the bridge and watched the cars speed by. I blew big pink bubbles the size of my face until the gum got stale and then spit it out through the fence at the semi-trucks beneath me. I ate all my necklaces and chewed on all the Tootsie Rolls at the center of the pops until my bag was empty. My mouth dry, my stomach happy, the sun setting, I decided I might as well see if there was something interesting happening at home. Besides, the thought of being alone on the bridge at night—without even a Bazooka Joe—had lost its thrill. I ran home.

When I arrived, my mom and the bridge ladies were in the same positions as when I left. And since they had not noticed my departure, I was going to make sure they noticed my arrival. I marched right over to my mom and put my sticky hand around her shoulder.

"Guess what, everybody? I just ran away. To Big Top." I announced it with flair and pride, my lips pale blue from the necklace candy. The ladies looked up from their cards and chuckled. I smiled back. I watched the cheeks of my mom's face turn pink. Then she grinned, patted my back, and told me we'd talk about it later.

We never did.

But I did feel the pain of her hand across my backside, a firm warning that I was never to wander off alone again, did I understand? What I had done was dangerous, risky, frightening, was that clear? Yes, it was as clear as the throbbing ache I felt when I tried to sit down for supper.

And so while the rest of the country was growing through historic civil rights rallies, student protests, and race riots; while my brothers biked and my father worked and my mother had long waved good-bye to her bridge ladies, I was getting scolded for exploring the suburbs of my neighborhood, bent on buying candy from a store with a circus-tent roof.

It was the first time I realized adventure could be dangerous.

I desired dragons with a profound desire. Of course, I in my timid body did not wish to have them in the neighborhood, intruding into my relatively safe world.

—J.R.R. Tolkien, *On Fairy-stories*

Though we might try to ignore it, discomfort is the uninvited companion on many adventures, isn't it? It hides behind bushes in the night, disguises itself in a variety of masks, or pounces on us when we have no idea anyone is around. It can work us over or prick our skin. But the hazards, risks, and resulting uneasiness don't go away, no matter how many times we close our eyes and wish them gone.

These days, merely reaching for the alarm clock confirms for me the ache that follows adventure. Muscles strained, head groggy, my body shivers from the absolute tension of living in a world where bullets fly into houses, cars crash on slow streets, and diseases invade friends' bodies, all while mothers are bathing their babies and neighbors are cooking hamburgers on the grill for their families.

Each morning, it seems we enter a sort of chaotic order, one where we are not safe, even if—or especially when—we believe in God. In fact, I think it is *because* God is God that I am uncomfortable each time I watch the evening news or read the local paper. I'd do things a little differently if I were in charge.

Yes, I'd prefer a painless journey, a faith that wasn't hard, and a life where simply stepping through the front door each night didn't have to feel like a miracle.

Of course, *that* would seem more like a funeral than an expedition, I reason with myself. Those of us who seek adventures must accept the dangers and conditions that accompany them. It's part of the deal, I realize, knowing that with each step, sharp rocks could stab our feet and make them bleed. Pirates could attack our ship. Serpents could chase us into a cave. Storms could wash out the trail. Friends could betray us. Anything could happen.

Which I know is better, far better, than nothing happening at all.

But it is not comfortable. Or safe. Still, I yield, because the older I get, the less I know for certain, except this: the risk of going is better than the peril of staying.

Maybe the rocks—or pirates or serpents or storms—keep reminding me to be all the more grateful for smooth roads or quiet seas. Maybe they whisper of a grander place, one where a glorious hand is more comforting than any earthly delusion of security. Maybe they feed my restless soul a healthy portion of purpose so that, most days, I want to lift my muscles off the mattress and step forward. All the while, I wonder why I'm privileged to have a mattress and a passport at all.

Each journey, though, could be costly. *To proceed despite risks.* It would not be passion or adventure without a price to pay.

> *In a dark time, the eye begins to see.*
> —Theodore Roethke

Instead of diving into the world with verve and confidence, I muddled through the next years after my Big Top adventure with ordinary suburban caution. If it was a softball game or a tennis match, I'd sweat only enough not to make a fool of myself, even if it meant losing, which it usually did. If it was an English class in high school or a cute boy sitting across the aisle, I'd turn in only half the assignments due and look away whenever the boy caught me staring. My efforts were careful, half-baked, good enough but never enough to do any good.

Self-protection ruled. Gray living.

And even though I'd learned about divine courage through a youth group I'd been a part of, sung the songs of hope and heaven with other teens, a different ache circulated through my blood by the time I left for college: emptiness. It pierced my neck and shoulders; it punched my stomach with self-conscious jabs. Nothing seemed right: no friendship I had, no outfit I wore, no team I joined. Ordinariness was suffocating.

"There was no emotion, not really, not strong and human," Miles told the aliens. What might have seemed like suburban comfort to others sometimes felt like suppression to me—or illusion—though I would not have used those words at the time.

I'd floundered through my first year of college when my father decided to give up the grayness of his suburban life with my mother. A month before what would have been their twenty-fifth wedding anniversary, he left. Shortly after they separated, my parents sold the only house I'd ever called home. My mom moved into a condominium lifestyle of loneliness and new jobs. I watched as she tried to recover, trying to pretend she could make it. Eventually, I think she did.

Divorce for my dad, I suppose, provided an alternative to that same stagnant feeling that had been chasing me. But divorce is never merely about ending a feeling, let alone a marriage, as if tearing up a piece of paper could sever a relationship. Nonetheless, he moved into an apartment in downtown Denver not far from the capitol, and I suddenly found myself wondering where I'd go for Thanksgiving and Christmas breaks. The ground was shifting beneath me.

I did the only rational thing I could think to do: I saved my paychecks and bought a plane ticket. I stalled my formal education and packed a bag instead. It didn't matter where I'd go, only that it was far from everything familiar, everything that hurt. Two friends planned a backpacking trip across England and Europe, and I invited myself along. We spent the first night in JFK Airport in New York, hoping to catch a standby flight in the morning. We arrived in London, took a ferry across to France, and rode the train all night to Florence, Italy. Each city we visited after that, we did not know where we would stay. Each time we were hungry, we did not know how to ask for food in the language of the locals.

But, you know, we never starved. Even when adventure becomes an escape, grace intervenes and keeps you moving.

As the snow began to fall, we found our way up the French Alps in Switzerland. The mountain beauty softened me; the travel soothed my emotional aches. There we listened to a short American man with a thin white beard dangling off his chin talk about God in human flesh. The man wore knickers, and though his hair was white, his eyes were clear and blue and alive. He'd started a Christian community called *L'Abri* (French for "shelter") in the tiny Swiss town where we decided to stay for a month or two; he'd written several books, and as a result, people from all over the world came to talk with him about "spiritual matters."

I had to confess, I'd never heard of this man named Francis Schaeffer before we arrived at L'Abri.

On a few starry nights, I listened to his complex ideas and theological certainties, but I did not understand him. In the daylight, I tried to read his books, but they did not draw me in. I did, however, begin to flip through the pages of another book this man kept referring to—the Bible. And for the next few weeks I devoured it like a woman who'd finally found refuge after too many days on the streets.

In each chapter or letter or account, I watched the man I'd heard of a few years before, the Christ, the Messiah, come into focus. I saw how he accepted the limitations of the Roman Empire as a working-class refugee, never losing sight of his treasure, never wandering from his mission. For days, I stared at his Story, caught in its grip, as this Nazarene carpenter confronted the evils of the time with his passion for love, for truth. He fought with words and kindness, traveled the lands with tenderness and savvy, embarked on treacherous journeys just to bring healing. I watched as he embraced the chaos of human life just so he could die.

On a cross.

And then one morning as I walked in freshly fallen snow, my head swirling with the words and tensions and aches of the past months, I wondered about this journey, about this God whom I'd never paid much attention to before now.

I'd been restless for sure, but I'd been alone as well. Wanting more. Hoping for more. Then I noticed an icicle dripping from a chalet, and in a whisper above the doubts, I remembered his claim in the Gospel of John: "I have come that they may have life, and have it to the full."

I stood still and stared hard at the Alps, watching shadows from the sun dance across the valley below. The snow was bright and the sky a dazzling blue. For some reason, a strange little song I had not sung in years emerged in my soul, and I began to hum: "Jesus loves me. This I know, for the Bible tells me so." It surprised me. The melody, the words, the certainty, each moved over me like a favorite story at bedtime. And suddenly, I felt more significant than I had in all my life.

The snow crunched beneath my boots as I marched back toward my chalet. The January cold felt fresh on my face, reminding me of winters in the Rockies. And though I was many thousands of miles from Colorado and the unfamiliar apartments where my parents now lived, and still full of restless fears and insecure dreams and everything but faith, I knew I had found home.

Or rather, he found me. Sometimes when you think you're taking one adventure, you stumble onto another.

> *I would rather be ashes than dust! I would rather that my spark should burn out in a brilliant blaze than it should be stifled by dry-rot. I would rather be a superb meteor, every atom of me in magnificent glow, than a sleepy and permanent planet. The proper function of man is to live, not to exist. I shall not waste my days in trying to prolong them. I shall use my time.*
>
> —Jack London, *Jack London's Tales of Adventure*

I suppose the road home takes a different turn for each of us. For surely the attempt to live out our days with every atom of our being is as unique as the atoms themselves. We are led not by a formula but by a destination.

That snowy walk almost twenty-five years ago tipped an avalanche of adventures for me that never once made me regret the trip or the time spent. Maybe the path really started earlier when I wandered off to Big Top. But I suspect it was even before that. Now I've come to see that in both and in between, in fantastic explorations and in stupid choices, the divine author known for centuries as the Word has plotted my journeys. Each detail carefully placed, each description beautifully arranged, each exclamation mark appearing at just the right time to transform an ordinary story into an exhilarating voyage.

This does not mean, however, that today I am filled with constant poise every time I step onto a plane or move to a different city. Nor does it keep me from sitting passively when I should be walking. I wish it did. It only means that the times I've reached into my pocket for directions I've usually been taken for a wild ride—the adventure of passion—found in the places I would never have thought to look.

Like New York City. It was adventure that first took me to this small island at the center of the world—even before I was in college (but that's a story for the next chapter). I marveled at the constant discoveries I met on the streets and yet trembled at their sheer scale. Every time I encountered a different culture, heard a cab honking, smelled a hot-dog stand, or elbowed my way through the crowds, I knew I was *not* in anything familiar, like the suburbs. No, I was in New York City.

And I loved everything *un*ordinary about it. It was a romance worth the pursuit. Yet it became another unsettling lesson that the adventure of passion is rarely smooth.

I moved to Gotham shortly after my thirty-sixth birthday to do what a thousand other writers had done—pursue the Muse—hoping that some of their creative force would rub off on me. This city prided itself on both survival and achievement, on drama and dreams, on wealthy lives and world-class aesthetics. You could be a starving artist in New York City and get respect. In fact, you could be anything here, go anywhere. Every type of passion imaginable fueled this place; this city crammed emotion into every corner of its landscape. It was a natural fit for a restless soul.

But I never imagined the city to be vulnerable. The treasures of adventure—like those on a pirate's map—might be difficult to find, but that's because they're hidden and well protected. You never expect they will be found, let alone stolen.

I'd just finished a breakfast meeting with some friends in midtown Manhattan. It was a glorious fall morning when I said good-bye, hopped on my bicycle, and pedaled up Madison Avenue toward home just north of Central Park. Rush hour was rushing and dreams were flying all around me as I passed 57th Street and rode north. A traffic light turned red, and I squeezed the brake on my handlebar to stop. Just a few feet from my bike, a woman walked in slow motion across the street, her horrified eyes on the sky behind me, her face pale from what she saw.

I glanced over my shoulder. Thick white smoke mixed with the morning air, pouring out of silver buildings and stealing the blue of the sky. *Another bad fire in New York,* I thought, as the traffic light turned green and I rode through a still-summer-lush Central Park, behind the Metropolitan Museum of Art, and out the north end into my neighborhood.

When I walked into the apartment my husband and I shared, the phone was ringing. And for the next few hours, darkness blurred my vision, shredding the city I had come to love, shattering—again—the place I had called home.

I did the only rational thing I could think to do: I got back on my bike. I could not sit in my living room watching the television's burning images of the World Trade Center while begging God for mercy in the horror happening outside. Instead, I rode south, along Riverside Park and over to Broadway.

The chaos I'd seen in the September sky had fallen onto the city, and I watched a human mass, covered in white soot, move north again. Women in power suits walked barefoot, crying or coughing, their emotions frozen in another place. Tourists numbed by both the swirl of the city and the hell they'd just witnessed held one another's hands. Police officers directed traffic, and businessmen were carried along with the crowd, stunned by how enormously life could change in just a few minutes.

I listened to the most terrible silence I have ever heard, afraid of the measureless pain that hovered around us.

"Just keep moving, folks, keep moving," a woman in a blue uniform shouted.

The advice seemed profoundly wise, so I obeyed. I pedaled some more, offering water and companionship when I could and wondering just how we would all survive this shipwreck.

Then at the corner of Thompson and Houston Streets, I had to stop riding. An enormous statue of Jesus—with outstretched arms—looked down at me, and a sign the width of the Catholic cathedral above him read, "Peace to the World." I read the words aloud, over and over and over, looking him straight in the eye and reaching for something in the air, anything to hold on to.

But all I felt was a raw ache.

What happened next surprised me as much as anything ever had. As I stared at that statue, the story from the pages I'd first read in Switzerland, from history itself, began speaking to my soul. The image of another dark sky came to mind as I watched gray ashes smoldering in the sunlight. I stared at the face of Christ, and in my mind's eye I saw fists slamming into his chest, nails slicing his wrists and feet, sharp thorns rammed into his head as he choked on his last breaths of air.

The compass had been broken.

A gruesome death spilled onto this street corner where I stood enraptured. It was not like a religious experience or a spiritual vision. It was simply an acknowledgment, a moment of recognition on a road. Suddenly I saw that the only understanding for the despair around me—if there could be such a thing—was *this* passion.

"He was despised and rejected by men, a man of sorrows, and familiar with suffering."

Somehow I knew that the horror on this New York corner, this historic glimpse of hell, could never be explained with words or books or television reports. Political analyses or theological speculations could never address a loss so terrible and so profound.

I studied again the statue above me. The marble arms seemed to point to another place altogether. A place where tears were wiped away. Where ordinary lives reflected splendor. Where sin was redeemed even when it walked—or rode—down the street in helpless despair.

That, at least, is what I wanted to believe.

The bike beneath me teetered as I rode to my husband's office to make sure he was okay. I found him and his colleagues safely together, already caring for friends and strangers with water and kindness. I hugged him. I cried. Without saying a word, we both knew that living in New York City would never be the same.

But do you know what? It made us—and most New Yorkers—care more. Live more. Absolute strangers stopped me on the subway to make sure everyone in my world was all right. Neighbors who'd never before spoken kept each other company. Our collective grief turned us outward.

We risked more, helped more, and understood a little more of what it meant, really meant, to be alive.

We mustn't forget, even when we want to. And I want to.

The journeys we take, the events in this world, will always grab us and shake us each time we open our eyes. They're marked with risky, tricky bends by their very nature. Movement invites peril. But staying put is far worse.

Which is why, I guess, that ever since I was born—in a rather ordinary manner at that—I've looked for the road that would stir my soul and quicken my pulse. Sometimes I've discovered this passion in the cities where I've lived. Sometimes it emerged in the jobs I've had, the trips I've taken, or the relationships I shared, all of which have reminded me of the enormous privileges I enjoy. Because in each step, each failure, each signpost, I still find a paradox filled with anguish *and* awe, sorrow *and* solace, discomfort *and* delight.

Each *moves* me.

All the steps connect me to the story of the One who went before me on the adventure from beyond the ages, encouraging me to abandon the ordinary for the unbelievable—even when the sky literally is falling around me. To exist without *that* story seems to forgo living itself, even if I am still breathing.

So if believing in God is what you're interested in, I feel obligated to tell you that it's hardly comfortable. In fact, it's dangerous and exhilarating, exciting, and threatening, crazy and logical, because it's far better than anything I could cook up on my own. I'm prone to wander, after all.

*Great art teaches us to feel pleasure,
liking, disgust, and hatred at those things
which really are pleasant, likeable,
disgusting, and hateful.*
—Ralph C. Wood,
"*Shadowlands*," a review

art (ärt) [Middle English, from Old French, from Latin *ars, art-*; see *ar-* in Indo-European roots.] noun.

The conscious production or arrangement of sounds, colors, forms, movements, or other elements in **a manner that affects the sense of beauty.**

High quality of conception or execution, as found in works of beauty; aesthetic value. A field or category of art, such as music, ballet, or literature.

The products of human creativity.

TWO

Creative Lands

and the beauty I ache to see

Art washes away from the soul the dust of everyday life.
—Pablo Picasso

Though I have always believed it, only lately have I had the language to say it: tedious days need colors and lines. Hardened souls need melodies and poems. These are necessities for living, not luxuries. They take us to the place where anything is possible and impossible at the same time, where images intersect with meaning, and seeing requires more than mere sight.

In this creative place, our best is born. In this land of wonder, hope does its finest work.

But it is not an easy place to visit if our nurtured inclination is contrary, if no one helped us understand why a painting invites rather than confounds. Or perhaps the tools for art and creativity haven't stayed with us; our education was half-baked.

So we learn in other ways.

One morning I was on the subway. The occasion was a reunion of writing friends—which, given New York's historic role as Muse, could be anytime—and the day resembled most days in the "world capital": busy, brisk, alive. There's a reason they call it the city that never sleeps—every corner, building, or face you pass invites your attention. Staying awake is not merely a survival skill here; it is an alluring way of life.

Once I arrived in Penn Station, I marched toward the number 2 train that would take me to Forty-second Street. There I'd catch the shuttle across midtown before heading north on the number 6 to the Upper East Side. I hurried past the many global citizens who'd come here, found a place on the platform, and waited. (Hurrying and waiting are also common here.) The silver underground transport slowed into the station and screeched such a high note that I poked my fingers in my ears. The doors slid apart. People got off and scattered. Then people got on and found a seat or a spot to stand. I followed and walked right into a fourth-grade class on a field trip.

It was noisy with young life. Laughter, conversations, commotion wiggled around the car. Boys played musical chairs. Teachers tossed glares and commands in between sighs. Girls giggled and pointed.

I stood, gripping a metal pole, listening, watching, thinking of my reunion. Until one slight, dark-skinned girl drew me in like a good story. She sat away from the other children, next only to a plump girl whose sleepy head kept nodding forward. They were a sharp contrast of each other, and more different still from the other children who were now hollering or howling.

The dark-skinned girl, though, noticed no one or no sound. Instead, she was transported to another place entirely by—of all things—a poem. Panels of photographic advertisements, selling everything from dermatologists and college courses to television shows and grocery stores, are posted strategically above the seats on most New York subways. Some wise soul along the way decided commuters also needed inspiration and created a series of panels called "Poetry in Motion," which has ever since featured scads of old and new, good and bad, short and long poems. Right next to the ads.

As I hung on to my pole, I noticed the girl, her eyes fixed on the lines in the poem above her classmates. Over and over, she read the poem aloud as if the sound of her own voice sliding around the melody was the best music she'd heard all day. The words, the rhythm, the tone, maybe even the meaning, all formed a glow around her face as she concentrated and read and sang. She was absorbed. Delighted.

Smitten by love of language, awake to its possibilities.

I was actually sad when the subway came to a stop at Forty-second Street and I had to get off. Especially when the girl did not notice we'd stopped at all, but kept reciting her poem even as the doors slid open and I stepped into the crowd. Though she did not see me, still captivated by the words and their sounds, how could I not smile at her passion? For a child's sense of wonder is a glorious, contagious gift, one that neither leaves us as our bodies change nor disappoints us as we travel through the years. It whispers life behind every otherwise routine moment.

If we'll stay awake to hear it.

Art has something to do with the achievement of stillness in the midst of chaos. . . . I think that art has something to do with an arrest of attention in the midst of distraction.

—Saul Bellow, in *The Paris Review Interviews*

Let me back up.

The first time I visited New York City, I didn't sleep much. It was so wildly different from the culs-de-sac of my suburban neighborhood that every inch of me wanted to take in every inch of it. I was sixteen years old, an awkward high school junior, reveling in a week of independence from parents and classes with fifteen other students on spring break. I had spent most of the year so intent on selling brownies and raffle tickets to pay for the trip that I don't remember a single other thing from that school year.

Only New York. The smell of hickory coals in hot pretzel stands. The towering canyons of buildings. The homeless men in Times Square selling pencils. The perpetual honks of taxicabs. The shops and cafés and street vendors. The endless motion of humanity on the sidewalks.

I was smitten.

I was there with the art department from my high school. Each year—three teachers—I'll call them Mr. Arthur, Miss Jamison, and Mr. Bridges because I'm ashamed to admit I can't remember their names—sponsored what they called the Big Apple Tour; each year they'd plan a trip that included galleries, museums, and Broadway shows for the first fifteen students who signed up and could afford to pay the fare from Denver. Or who were willing to spend the majority of the school year working fund raisers to get the discount price. Like me. If I wanted to go to that strange city, my parents—who were hard at work in offices and stores—said they would pay half if I paid the rest.

That was all the incentive I needed.

The funny thing was I'd never enrolled in an art class. I'm sure I'd taken one once in elementary school, had someone hand me brushes and paints and say, "Here, Jo, this is blue and this is a canvas." I'm sure someone in junior high tried to teach me how to draw other shapes and mix colors to create illusions and perspective, but it never stayed with me. Besides, by the time I'd entered high school, I only wanted the creative company of friends to relieve some of the teen angst that had hit us all. What did it matter if I'd never taken a single painting or drawing class the high school offered?

Thankfully, Mr. Arthur said it didn't matter at all. I wasn't required to have any art experience for the trip because he said I would learn. It was easy to pick up, he assured me, like riding a bike or skiing. And because those activities *were* easy for me, I believed him. I just needed to keep up my fund raising payments through the year so I could go. It didn't take much to convince me. Something about these art teachers—the way they talked about the paintings we would see, the descriptions they gave of the galleries and museums—lured me into believing them. It woke up something in my dulled suburban bones.

We landed in March when the winter frost had not yet left the city. Wrapped in Colorado ski parkas, we descended from the airport bus onto Forty-fourth Street where we hurried toward our hotel in Times Square. The rooms were no bigger than the laundry-room in my family's basement back home, the bathroom barely wide enough to turn around in. Neither mattered to me; I wasn't planning to spend much time here anyway.

Our first stop was the Metropolitan Museum of Art on Fifth Avenue. Mr. Bridges handed us a map of the exhibits throughout the massive building, pointed toward the steps and hallways beyond the lobby, and told us to meet back at the visitors' booth in four hours. Then he and the other teachers, along with the smart students and their friends, scattered quickly. I wanted to follow them, to see what they saw, to understand how this stuff with colors and shapes and lines worked. I wanted to know their secret. But I just stood there, watching them move through the place with the same eagerness I'd seen in fans at sporting events.

Other people hurried by too. Groups of schoolchildren on field trips and senior citizens on tours wandered past me with their guides. They all looked excited, nodding their heads and pointing, enthusiasm widening their eyes as if this was the Christmas of a lifetime. I noticed a few tourists with cameras around their necks standing and gawking nearby. They were speaking Japanese and reading their museum maps in the same language. I glanced down at mine, and though it was in English, it might as well have been the same as theirs. I needed a translator.

I studied the various sections and lists of exhibits in my map. Should I visit the American Paintings and Sculptures, the section with Drawings and Prints, the Egyptian or Asian Art, or the Arts of Africa, Oceania, and the Americas? Or maybe I should go see the European Sculpture and Decorative Arts? What about the really old stuff from Greece, Etruria, Cyprus, and Roman settlements, which, as the brochure said, included "marble, bronze, and terracotta sculpture, vases, wall paintings, jewelry, gems, glass, and utilitarian objects"? And what of the wings and halls where the costumes, armor, and furniture were exhibited?

I felt dizzy.

So I ducked into the gift shop. I bought a postcard. I glanced through a big thick book full of pictures of paintings in the Modern Art section and tried to interpret what I saw as scribbles and caricatures and cartoons. I looked harder, reading the captions even. But nothing clicked. I turned the page. More squiggles and oddities. I sighed and closed the book, careful not to damage it. Then I bought a Pepsi in the café, watched other tourists as they asked security guards where the contemporary photographs or European exhibits were, and even pulled out a pen from my backpack to write a note on my postcard. I strolled outside and down the majestic steps of the Met, circled the fountains beside it, and watched the taxis and buses on Fifth Avenue. I bought a pretzel and felt the cold March air on my cheeks. A street magician drew a crowd on the sidewalk with his juggling act, and I applauded with the others before climbing the steps back up to the museum and finding a seat by the visitors' booth.

When Mr. Arthur and the others finally appeared, their faces glowed with a rosiness that made me wonder if they'd somehow slipped by me and gone outside like I had. But the brochures, the tablets of notes, and the prints of pictures in their hands suggested otherwise.

"Wasn't it great? Did you see Bronzino's *Portrait of a Young Man*?"

"And the *Madonna and Child*?"

"And the Manet collection?"

"Glorious."

"Amazing."

"Brilliant."

I smiled and nodded, like I knew what they were talking about. Other students gathered around, nodding and laughing as if their team had just scored a touchdown, and Mr. Bridges glanced at his watch before taking a quick head count. Their collective enthusiasm rose. The banter swelled. Even as we descended the steps and boarded a bus that took us to the Museum of Modern Art where the excitement of our group climbed to new heights, my confusion only intensified. Over the next few days, as we stopped at other museums and galleries, at Saint Patrick's Cathedral and the Rockefeller Center, at the Statue of Liberty and Broadway, and until finally we boarded a plane and flew back to Colorado, I struggled to keep up. To understand the whirlwind of sights and shapes and colors. I watched as the others interpreted each with ease.

I wish I could say that I understood even a dash of what happened at the Met and the galleries on that trip. Or that my education in the fine arts was profoundly influenced by that first introduction to the great works housed at New York's most famous museums. I wish I had been moved in some way. But I simply didn't know what to make of the paintings and statues I saw. No matter how much I wanted to admire them like my teachers and peers had, I just didn't know what all the fuss was about.

Back home, when my parents asked me about the art trip to New York, I shrugged. I muttered something about how I thought the churches were nice, the theater was fun, and the city was big. They waited for more, but I didn't know what to say. Not much else about the tour registered, let alone found words.

Which is probably why I still couldn't tell you the names of those high school art teachers.

> I sculpt and paint to give permanence to my feelings about how terrible this world truly is. Nothing is real to me except my own feelings; nothing is true except my own feelings as I see them all around me in my sculptures and paintings. I know these feelings are true, because if they are not true they would make art that is as terrible as the world.
>
> —Chaim Potok, *My Name Is Asher Lev*

I wish it had made sense. I wish some clues about shades and shapes had taken root in my heart and sprouted beautiful paintings. Instead, I grew distracted by the memories of homeless people and their pencils in Times Square, the lights on the theater marquees, and the masses of people—all types of people from all types of places—that passed us on the sidewalk. Each face astonishingly different, each story mysterious.

These were the memories that stayed with me from that first authentic encounter with art—the breathing, walking creativity that bumped into me on the street. But noticing them meant I missed the meaning of the pictures that hung on the walls at the museums. Which led me to believe that I did not belong to this community of artists. Secretly, of course, I wanted to admire the drawings, sculptures, paintings. They seemed magnetic and held something I knew I did not have. After that time at the Met, I tried to avoid them. I pushed away the idea of anything I couldn't understand. I figured the hands and souls that created them were uniquely gifted with a purpose and a place I would never be a part of.

They were born that way, people said, blessed with great talents. You'll find yours someday. So I went looking.

Or that's what I told myself I was doing. A few years after high school—the same months my parents were divorcing when I was backpacking in Europe—I decided to give the art thing another chance. Maybe it was the beauty of the wintry Swiss Alps or the new discovery I'd made about the Maker of these mountains. Or both. I was becoming curious again.

Wonder pulled. My soul, I suppose, was thawing. That was the only reason I could see for saying yes one January morning when Marti, my backpacking friend, asked if I'd catch the train with her to Florence, Italy, so she could see where "it" all started.

"Where what started?" I asked.

"*What?!* Are you crazy?" She couldn't help herself. We were crunching through the snow of this quiet mountain village, and Marti's enthusiasm took me to my art teachers in New York. "See the paintings, the statues, you know, the place where it began. The Renaissance, that's what!"

I counted the little money I had left, found my Eurail discount pass, and agreed it couldn't hurt. She rolled her eyes, and by the next week we'd arrived in Firenze with the name of a cheap pension and a map to the Palazzo Vecchio—the town hall. The brochure called it the most impressive in Tuscany: "Overlooking the Piazza della Signoria with its famous *David* statue as well as the gallery of statues in the adjacent Loggia dei Lanzi, it is one of the most significant public places in Italy." I shrugged as I read, aware of my tourist status in more than geographic terms, but I couldn't argue with the excitement of my friend. We dropped off our backpacks and rushed toward the square.

There was a line. A long one. Dozens of other visitors stood outside the building known as Galleria dell'Accademia, wrapped around the corner spilling onto the next street, waiting for a glimpse into the Tribuna. We found the end, entered the queue, and shuffled forward slowly with the crowd. A barrage of questions crammed my head as I studied the faces and sizes of the people around me. Marti interrupted with facts and figures from the tour book she was poring over. I'd nod my head, trying to appear interested.

Finally we came to the entry where a small uniformed guard ushered us in. It was quiet and cold, the same cavernous feeling as in New York's Saint Patrick's Cathedral. But the stone walls were unlike any I'd seen anywhere else. There was nothing like this where I came from. And I still wasn't sure what I was doing here.

Then we saw him. *David*. Michelangelo's statue, standing naked and gray and tall in the Tribuna that had been built especially to house it. I stopped still.

I did not know what to make of him. The seventeen-foot marble likeness of this biblical king stood suave and noble, confident and muscular, apparently caught just at the moment he decided to do battle with Goliath. A tour guide said that it had taken Michelangelo three years to finish his masterpiece, that he had used the artistic discipline known as *disegno*. *Disegno*, she continued, was considered the finest form of art at that time. Not only did it mimic the holy act of creation, it elevated the male human form to godlike proportions. It also meant that the artist believed the image was already in the block of stone he was working on—much as the human soul was found within the physical body. In *David*'s case, though, the proportions were not quite true to form. The virtues of universal man—his physical strength and intellectual reasoning—were found in Michelangelo's representation of David. The tour guide claimed that "the entire work was a perfect synthesis of the Florentine Renaissance."

Her words might as well have been in Japanese—no language was going to help me make sense of this. All I could do was stare: the veins in his arms, the slingshot on his shoulder, the furrow of his brow, even his nostrils and penis and stomach muscles and toenails, all revealed some*thing* I had no words for. *David* confounded me; he numbed me and pierced me at the same time. He was so . . . big.

When we finally stumbled out into the plaza, Marti rambled on and on about the sculpture we'd just seen, mentioning every detail, trait, and artistic factoid she knew. Once she caught her breath, she turned to me and asked what I thought. I wanted to tell her that I understood what she'd been talking about, that this world of chiseled marble and old art and stunning beauty was one I'd easily navigated and defined long ago.

Instead, I simply shook my head and looked at a pigeon. I felt even more like a tourist, an outsider, than I had when our trip began. And though I'm sure Marti dragged me around to many other galleries in Firenze that week and told me dozens of other facts about the dozens of other statues, paintings, and buildings I'm sure we saw, there was only one I remembered.

Often while reading a book one feels that the author would have preferred to paint rather than write; one can sense the pleasure he derives from describing a landscape or a person, as if he were painting what he is saying, because deep in his heart he would have preferred to use brushes and colors.

—Pablo Picasso

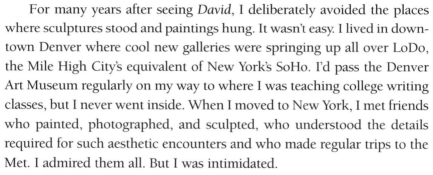

For many years after seeing *David*, I deliberately avoided the places where sculptures stood and paintings hung. It wasn't easy. I lived in downtown Denver where cool new galleries were springing up all over LoDo, the Mile High City's equivalent of New York's SoHo. I'd pass the Denver Art Museum regularly on my way to where I was teaching college writing classes, but I never went inside. When I moved to New York, I met friends who painted, photographed, and sculpted, who understood the details required for such aesthetic encounters and who made regular trips to the Met. I admired them all. But I was intimidated.

So I read books. I wrote profiles and journalism and such. I watched movies and went to plays because these were stories, and I could understand them. I began to question the creative process, what to do with it, how to harness it, why we had it at all. Did it extend beyond a painter's canvas? Was it more than a chiseled piece of marble with lifelike veins? Or was it exclusive and protected by and for a chosen few who could either afford it or comprehend it?

I talked with people and listened to sermons, though not many pulpits considered this Sunday morning material. Some people told me artist types were indeed a strange breed who lived on the fringe of acceptability, served no useful purpose, and lived far from where the rest of us normal folks lived and moved and had our beings. Others called artists nothing short of prophets—in the same league as Isaiah or Paul—a gifted lot who could speak truth at the same time they critiqued the culture and its people with the mere stroke of a brush.

It was as if each of these two had no room for the other.

So one morning in New York, I suppose when I saw a child reading a subway poem or when a friend helped me make sense of a painting at the Met, I peeked at my fear. The pull in my soul said there was something more. Had to be more. Revealed in the chase of wonder. In that feeling that happens every time we stumble upon a marvel so surprising, a joy so unexpected, that we cannot explain why our tired soul and achy bones suddenly feel young again.

It was something I'd experienced even without words, something I needed if I was going to stay awake through this earthly existence. Something I needed in order to breathe and bleed and feel—even if my attempts at understanding or creating were raw and primitive. Even if I had millions of dollars or only one in my bank account, if I lived in a Western country or a developing one. This seemed to be my DNA, to be everyone's, in fact.

Creative because we were first created.

Then I went to Ireland . . . and it was as though Home had come alive. Its vitality was inexhaustible, yet it was rhythmical, alliterative, formal, always on the point of bursting into poetry.

—George Thomson, from Blasket Island Centre exhibit

A week before I was introduced to the man I'd eventually marry, I flew from New York with five other single women across the Atlantic. For seven straight days, we pooled our resources to bicycle around Ireland's Dingle peninsula on the southwestern coast.

My thirty-seven-year-old body was not necessarily up for the challenge. Though I'd grown up around softball fields and ski slopes, had played soccer until I was thirty-five, my muscles and joints by then had worn down, and a premature case of arthritis had set in. A bicycle became new legs for me. And because my pride as an athlete had not deteriorated—though my hip had—I never hesitated in saying yes to biking.

We landed in Shannon Airport and took the bus toward County Clare. We met our local guide, recovered from jet lag, and after eggs and sausage, we began to ride. The air was fresh and soft, the paths lush and satisfying. Each day was filled with miles and miles of green glory and hilly challenges. Each morning I awoke fantastically tired, simultaneously exhausted and inspired in words I could not find. I'd push the limits of aching limbs and battered muscles, ignoring the shooting pains each time I made it to the top of a mountain pass I never expected to conquer. I'd grimace beyond the soreness, despite the wind and the rain, and I'd keep pedaling, searching for a vocabulary that would do justice to the experience, falling short with every attempt.

We were here on the Emerald Isle, after all, and though inept at expression, we were determined to catch its charm each time we stopped at an abandoned castle or church, each moment we rested our wondrously tired beings in villages or pubs. Ireland's dark lager, they say, is good for you.

By day four, with skies typically gray yet luminous, muscles and joints throbbing, language waning, we pushed our way out to the daunting ledge of the coast. On one side of our ride was the endlessness of the Atlantic; on the other were hills and pastures so colorfully detailed I wasn't always sure they were real. We cut in front of the rain, rounded a valley, and finally arrived in a village speckled only by a single pub, a few farms, and of all things, a museum.

I wasn't sure what to make of it.

The words by the English scholar George Thomson had been chiseled across the entrance of this lonely museum. Considering we'd just traveled beside some of nature's most captivating but uncapturable "poems," his words were familiar, like a song that resonated though I'd never before heard it. I stared and read, amazed at his choice. More amazed still when I strolled into the entrance and discovered where I was.

This was the Blasket Island Centre, a unique building that celebrated not the glorious terrain or the political landscape of the country, not even its religious heritage, though Ireland was abounding in each. The Centre's sole purpose was to honor some of the country's most rugged writers, artists, and poets as well as the creative expressions that literally helped them survive.

It was the farthest western point of our trip and the last place I expected to be taught a lesson on the significance of creativity. Outside the door, the clouds had descended, soaking our bikes in the parking lot. The ocean (with an American land far beyond it) glared at us from one direction. The other revealed a tiny island called Blasket, three miles across the bay. On this island, remarkable poetic writing—rhythmical, alliterative, formal—emerged from a relatively normal lot of farmers and fishermen who were extraordinarily rich in creative expression.

I borrowed a pen and paper from the lady at the information booth. And I wandered slowly through the exhibit.

Afflicted by both the mighty mood swings of the ocean and the political climate of the land, the islanders, as they came to be called, believed their survival depended on being alert: alert to each other, to the sounds of thunder, the looming dark skies, and the salty winds that determined their daily activities. Every change in a day's weather from morning to night, from spring to winter, meant life—or death—for the small village of 150 rosy-cheeked folks.

Consequently, they were an enormously creative community, I discovered as I roamed the Centre, staring at enlarged black-and-white photographs that hung from the ceilings or at musical instruments and agricultural artifacts in glass cases. These people *had* to pay attention to the stuff of living. They had no formal education to rely on; they didn't learn to write until Thomson and others visited and taught them as adults.

Their lives were wide awake.

The poet John Millington Synge had been the first of the island's distinguished visitors in 1905, snapping shots of the place with a box camera. He was as much a mystery to them as they were to him, for the islanders barely knew of a world beyond theirs. To them, fishing, potatoes, stories, songs, and life together, mixed with an occasional venture to Sunday church across the bay, weather permitting, were all they knew and all that mattered.

I could see why. Here nature fed creativity. The scenes themselves were always on the point of bursting into poetry. The hills and waves breaking against jagged cliffs provided a steady diet of inspiration for the islanders. The sea gave both daily sustenance and a healthy dose of terror and admiration, what Thomson called a "deep-seated belief in the kinship of man and nature, both subject to the same cycle of day and night, summer and winter, birth and death," a theme that persisted in Irish poetry through the ages.

And so they stayed awake and wrote what they saw. Not pithy captions of sentimental nature scenes but words of art and substance and *inexhaustible vitality*. Like this from Muiris O'Suilleabhain, born in 1904, dead by 1950:

> It was a beautiful morning, a streak of light across Cnoc-a-choma in the east and life coming into everything. The sheep which had been sitting in the furrow in the run of the night arose and stretched itself. The

folded leaf was opening. The hen which had hidden her head under wings was crying gob-gob-gob to be let out in the fields. Bird, beast and man were awaking to pay homage to the sun.

Like this from Peig Sayers, 1873–1958:

I sat down on the bank above the beach where I had a splendid view around me. Dead indeed is the heart from which the balmy air of the sea cannot banish sorrow and grief.

And this from the island's most famous artist, fisherman, and farmer, Tomas O'Crohan, 1855–1937:

A misty white haze rose from the sea at this time floating over the round-topped hills. The plants on the hillside were not without their own sweet scent. You need not stir from where you stood on the height to fill your lungs with the scented breeze from whichever direction it might be blowing. I used to wonder why city folk would make for a place like this, but I need not have wondered.

Like the others, O'Crohan was determined to capture life, as he wrote, with "high literary merit coming out of an oral culture, triumphs of determination to master the written word, to leave a record of what life was like in my time and the neighbors that lived with me."

That life also included playing music on instruments the islanders crafted themselves. Sculpting furniture from driftwood. Harvesting potatoes and onions. Telling stories. Laughing, remembering, listening. In between growing, catching, and preparing their meals. Together.

The islanders lived during a time, it occurred to me as I walked through their memorial, when C. S. Lewis, J. R. R. Tolkien, and a few other writers who called themselves the Inklings were gathering around their own creative works across the Channel in Oxford. From the early 1900s to the time the Blasket Island was abandoned in 1953—human survival had met its match—these undereducated yet dramatically artistic fishermen and fisherwomen produced nearly twenty-five remarkable books of fiction, biography, and poetry written in Irish (Gaelic) and now translated into several languages. They were Inklings too.

Inspired for the sake of survival and of living well in a terrain that challenged both, the islanders often told the tale of the woman who had never stirred from her home. On her first venture, coming to the crest of the pass and gazing over the spreading landscape, she cried out, "What a wide, weary place is Ireland!" Frightened by the vastness of the revealed world, she turned back forever to her cozy, familiar island.

I shook my head as I finally made my way toward my bike, the rain still pouring, my friends impatient with my meandering, my body sore. Yet I was anything but tired. For here, at the edge of the sea, I discovered a community of writers and artists who could not help but create, who nourished one another—and foreign admirers like me.

I don't know if it was the rain, the story I'd just discovered, or the combination of the creative nature in each, but the hills looked more magical after that. The air seemed fresher, and my legs felt stronger the rest of the trip. Everywhere I looked—and smelled and listened—I saw poems. And I saw art.

> *Wonder is the normal response to splendor. This is why the best of scholars and teachers share in their separate disciplines a common trait, an indispensable characteristic, namely, that of marveling at reality, of looking for explanations and causes. Their classes come alive. . . . Beauty is crucial to the human enterprise because it triggers wonder.*
> —Thomas Dubay, SM, *The Evidential Power of Beauty: Science and Theology Meet*

And so this trail of wonder has led me to a curious gratitude for an artist's work, to a place where I see that the creative process must be honored as a divine one. Though I've not been given a block of stone to chisel into a statue, I'm beginning to understand—between the subway poems and the Irish hills—that words, ideas, and language are also laced with an artist's soul.

I am no longer an outsider. I am simply a different type of artist. Included by the Word made flesh.

Why do my palms grow clammy when I say that?

Maybe because I now know what happens when I reach for a pencil or a paintbrush to form images that look no different from the pictures I might have created in the classes I can't remember. It does not matter anymore. Watching the water dry through the colors is enough.

Maybe it is precisely because of my picture-less paintings that I am enchanted by art's power. How *did* he do that, I ask, hypnotized by Jules Bastien-Lepage's painting of Joan of Arc above my desk. Her hand is stretched out to nothing, but her face—like the garden where she stands—is so full of *something*. So reflective of another world, of that other land far from this one. So overflowing with life, power, and beauty in one grand image that I keep staring. And I must remember to breathe.

It is *this* wonder of art—and the art of wonder—that keeps us awake, that traps our emotions in the middle of our throats, that deepens the color in our daily routines. Because whether in music, theater, paintings, films, or stories, art reminds us our hearts are still beating. One friend of mine goes so far as to say—with great passion, I might add—*art saves lives*. I do not doubt her.

In fact, I suspect *that* was what was happening for me when I was young and gobbling up books at bedtime. Or when I returned from my New York spring break in high school and slapped teen magazine pictures with Elmer's glue across my bedroom wall to form a glossy collage (pity the next owners of the house). Or when I picked up a guitar and plucked out sounds I was sure were songs. Or when I filled pages and pages of journals with feelings, poems, and stories and then pretended I never wanted anyone to read them.

It happened again when I saw an astonishing Broadway play, when I cooked a really good meal, or listened—really listened—to a symphony. When I wrote my first novel and when I stared at a painting like *Joan of Arc* or the hills of Ireland or the muscles of *David* until I could begin to see . . . *some thing*.

I was being saved. Over and again. And the longer I live, the more saving I need.

Think you it was for such a life that this good arm was fixed upon my shoulder, or that head placed upon your neck? There is work in the world, man, and it is not by hiding behind stone walls that we shall do it.
—Sir Arthur Conan Doyle,
The White Company

vo·ca·tion (vō-kā´shən) [Middle English vocacioun, *divine call to a religious life,* from Old French *vocation* from Latin vocatio, vocation—*a calling.*] noun.

A regular **occupation**, especially one for which a person is particularly suited or qualified.

An inclination, as if **in response to a summons**, to undertake a certain kind of work, especially a religious career; a calling.

Three

Working Ways

and the jobs I cannot keep

I'd rather not sing than sing quiet.
—Janis Joplin

I picked up the Classifieds section of the newspaper yesterday. For reasons not entirely clear, it's a habit I formed long ago, this scouring the pages for *help wanted*. Like most days, yesterday's lists held scads of possibilities: everything from advertising director and kindergarten teacher to restaurant server and strategic life coach. A photographer needed an apprentice, a radio producer was looking for an assistant, and a youth center was desperate for an activities director.

I sighed. Then I recycled the paper and turned on the computer. But like a ghost moving through me, I instinctively reached for my surfboard and clicked my way to an ocean of employment sites. A public relations firm near the town where I live needed a media specialist, a college administrator needed a savvy right arm, and a security company needed a dispatcher. My imagination rode the wave of each until I slipped and was dumped onto some cyber-shore called Monster Jobs.

Monster Jobs? Were they serious? What could they possibly be looking for? Three-headed giants to run companies? New creatures to rise from the sea? I shifted uneasily. Was this the latest answer to the age-old question: how do we *really* feel about work? Like it's a shuffling scary ogre that must be endured? The bigger and uglier, the better?

I shut down.

I've never understood how to walk beside the ogres and monsters of this career-driven culture, so rife with fire-breathing options and man-eating standards. I've never quite figured out how to blow fresh air into buried dreams or pull out maidenly features to win the favor of some boss-king. Sure, I could do practical things, like dust off my résumé and send it to that PR firm. I could revisit an old fantasy for radio and call that producer or venture into a new land altogether as an apprentice to a photographer. I *could.* But the *should* whispering from my shoulder draws gigantic question marks in my soul.

And so the cautions of culture linger long in this place called vocation. In this necessary world of winning wages and paying taxes. Which I suppose is why I read dozens of ads. And I ask, What *should* I do to earn a living? Why is living something to be earned anyway? How come *this* road feels so bumpy, so dangerous? So littered with ghosts and daggers, tricks and treasures?

Why is it so hard to know what to do with our lives?

The question prods me daily. But so far I have not found many answers in the Classifieds section.

I wonder if I've been changed in the night? Let me think: was I the same when I got up this morning? I almost think I can remember feeling a little different. But if I'm not the same, the next question is, Who in the world am I? Ah, that's the great puzzle!

—Alice, in *Alice's Adventures in Wonderland* by Lewis Carroll

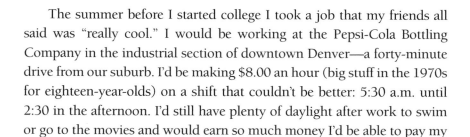

The summer before I started college I took a job that my friends all said was "really cool." I would be working at the Pepsi-Cola Bottling Company in the industrial section of downtown Denver—a forty-minute drive from our suburb. I'd be making $8.00 an hour (big stuff in the 1970s for eighteen-year-olds) on a shift that couldn't be better: 5:30 a.m. until 2:30 in the afternoon. I'd still have plenty of daylight after work to swim or go to the movies and would earn so much money I'd be able to pay my part of the tuition bills. I'd probably also be able to buy a new car.

Dollar signs can make even the simplest child delusional.

I'd already had other jobs before landing this prize—work, I was sure, that had prepared me for any task. My first in high school, for instance, was as a part-time clerk in the snack bar of a major department store, making popcorn, cleaning coffeepots, and turning hot dogs on one of those hot metal steam-grills so they wouldn't shrivel or burn. (This was before the invention of fancy machines that rotated hot dogs by themselves.) I was good at it. Plus, I got all the popcorn I wanted as well as a discount on jeans and shampoo at the store, so the work never seemed so bad.

My second was as a carhop at an A&W Root Beer Drive-In, a leftover from the drive-in rage of the 1960s. A friend from school told me her family owned the restaurant/soda fountain and if I ever needed a job, her mom would hire me. "Besides, the tips are great," she said. I didn't need convincing. It was the summer before my last year of high school, and I brought eight months experience with me from the snack bar. Stylish in a uniform of brown polyester pants and a bright orange top with the A&W logo on my chest, I'd show up for each shift, dump French fries in plastic baskets and ice cream in mugs and then hang trays from the side of half-opened windows on customers' cars. I made change from a metal coin dispenser I wore on a belt. I felt significant. And my friend was right: the tips were great.

Until I spilled an entire root beer float on a man in a three-piece suit. In ninety-five-degree summer heat. The tray didn't quite catch on the window, and the mugs on top of it flipped over onto the driver's seat. He was sticky and unhappy and not at all interested in tips.

I never went back.

After that, I figured how hard could a job at the Pepsi-Cola Bottling Company be? My father worked as a vice president there, which meant I didn't really have to fill out an application. I did, though, because he told me to. The last thing he wanted was for permanent employees to think his daughter was above the rules, even if she was there only for the summer. Before she went on to college. To get a degree in secondary education. So she could teach high school kids. And make him proud.

I wasn't sure yet what subject I'd teach, but somewhere along the way—probably because of teachers like Mrs. Manning or Mr. Archibeque—I decided it was the best career choice for me. I didn't want to be a secretary or a housewife, and the only other choice seemed to be a teacher. Yes, that's what I'd become. A seed of a dream for my own classroom had even begun to take root in my soul. Teachers could make a difference, I thought. They mattered. They were smart. I wanted in.

Before that could happen, though, I'd spend the summer in the really cool job at Pepsi-Cola. So I filled out all the forms, met my supervisor in the factory, and sat through an equal opportunity training session. I was given a key to a locker and shown where to punch my time card. It was all very exciting.

I slapped my alarm at 4:15 that first morning, stumbled to the shower, and thirty minutes later planted my body behind the steering wheel of my Volkswagen Bug. No one was on the road at that time so the drive was easy and smooth—what I remembered of it. I parked across from the factory and found my way into the locker room, where I slipped on a one-piece jump suit. Someone handed me a hard hat and thick plastic safety glasses, and told me to stand near a certain spot next to a conveyer belt.

The noise hurt my ears. Trucks were revving up around me. Machinery in full throttle was sending cardboard boxes in wooden crates screeching past me on the belt. Around turns and up inclines the crates moved, jolted along by silver rollers that reminded me of the hot-dog grill. Eventually, the crates arrived at a spot where they were stabilized for a few seconds while metal arms dropped glass bottles of Dr. Pepper or Pepsi-Cola into them. Then the conveyer belt rammed the boxes to a huge trough where workers like me took them off and put them in a neat pile for forklift tractors to move them somewhere else.

I stood with others in the noise. About ten other workers, mostly women, wearing jumpsuits and hard hats, moved robotically around the waist-high conveyor belt. Every thirty minutes or so, we stepped to a new spot around the belt, loading it with boxes, unfolding cartons, or stacking crates. The rotation of our positions, I heard later, was intended to fight the tedium of the tasks. It was too loud to talk with anyone, and if you tried, you had to yell and no one could understand you anyway. I tried to sing but couldn't hear myself. I tried to pray but was too groggy. It was only six in the morning, a part of the "cool" equation I hadn't factored in.

Three hours later, shoulders stiff and forehead sweaty, I sat in a windowless employee lounge for break surrounded only by vending machines and refrigerators. Plastic tables and chairs were scattered atop the concrete floor. A thick, brown-haired woman in her fifties grabbed something from the fridge, found a table by herself, and sat muttering and crunching popcorn. A group of other women descended on a table across the room, exchanging coffee thermoses and gossip like they were at a picnic.

I bought a wrapped pastry-thing from a machine and sat down with the popcorn woman. I asked her name.

"Annabell. Annabell, that's it, my name," she said without looking up and without asking mine. I told her anyway. Someone across the room yelled. Annabell crunched. A radio blared. I'd barely finished unwrapping my pastry-thing when a whistle blew. Annabell and the others automatically pushed out their chairs and darted back to the conveyor belt. Some took candy bars with them, so I shoved my breakfast into my jumpsuit pocket and followed.

For the rest of the day, I stood and rotated, unfolded cartons and pulled off crates, stacked and sweated, and sighed a lot. I watched Annabell mutter and the other women yawn or throw things or go through the same motions I was going through. Every half hour or so, I'd look at the clock high on the wall and dream about how soon I'd be driving home. Going swimming. Seeing my friends.

I'd escape in my mind to a bright room with windows, desks, students, and a chalkboard. Watching the image grow, I'd occupy more of it throughout the day, in between mutters and rotations, bottles rattling and trucks grinding.

That night when my dad asked how the first day went, I shook my head from side to side—a buzz still vibrating in between—and complained about the heat, the stiffness, and, of course, the noise. He nodded and said something about gratitude as he finished his spaghetti and read the newspaper. I looked at him and cleared the dishes. And I fell asleep before the *Tonight Show with Johnny Carson.*

The next few mornings came earlier and earlier. My bed was softer and the room more peaceful than I'd ever noticed before. Until my dad would knock on my door after my alarm clock had gone off. I'd drag myself out, get into my VW, and find my stupid hard hat in my locker as I got ready for another round of rotations, crates, and racket. Then something happened. Rather, *nothing* happened, and that made all the difference.

Gradually, during the next couple of weeks, I started drinking Dr. Pepper for breakfast. I began muttering to myself under the noise about boxes or popcorn or whatever, as I'd seen Annabell do. And I was no longer looking at the clock so much to fantasize about what I'd do after work as to wait for the times my supervisor would tap my shoulder and point me to a new spot around the conveyor belt. The trucks' gears had become background noise and the machinery a dull buzz.

The work didn't seem so bad.

The leader of the hard hats sat beside me one day at lunch in the windowless lounge. I unwrapped my sandwich and took a bite. She tried to make small talk, wanted to know why I was working at Pepsi-Cola in the factory when my dad was in the office.

"I'm saving for college in the fall," I said.

She nodded for more. I continued.

"I'm going to be a teacher." I lifted my shoulders proudly and remembered my classroom. Her eyebrow rose slightly.

"Is that right?" she said, pouring what looked like thin tar from a thermos into a plastic mug.

"Yup, that's right. High school, probably language arts or something like that. Maybe I'll even coach a sport."

"Why would you want to do that?"

I swallowed. "Why?"

"Yeah, why?" She gulped her tarlike liquid and didn't wait for my answer. "You'll never find a job. Don't you know how hard it is just to get hired? For every one classroom these days, there's a hundred teachers waiting in line."

"Well, I, uh—"

"Trust me. And even if you were one of the lucky ones, you'd never make any money."

I set down my sandwich. "Teaching isn't about—"

But what she did next startled me so much I couldn't finish my sentence: she plopped her elbow on the table, leaned toward me, and pointed her index finger directly between my eyes. She narrowed hers and firmed her lips.

"I ought to know what I'm talkin' about. I was a high school history teacher for fourteen years. They push you around from school to school, and they don't pay you enough to live on, let alone feed yourself. It's not worth it." She kept pointing. "And you think kids today even want to learn? Trust me, you do *not* want to be a teacher."

"Yes, I—"

"You'd make better money and benefits staying here. Doing this." She took a sip and said, "Working at Pepsi is ten times better than teaching ever could be. Besides, you'll *never* get a job."

I blinked. Sweat had gathered across my forehead, and I dabbed it with my napkin. Finally, her words found some meaning in my mind. I shifted. And then *I* leaned forward.

But I couldn't bring myself to say what I was thinking: Pepsi over teaching? A factory instead of a school? Dr. Pepper instead of students? How could it be? This woman sitting across from me in her jumpsuit, waving her finger at me, had abandoned her very own classroom to unfold cartons and put them in crates just so she could make more money? And benefits?

Suddenly a paycheck seemed as invasive to me as an alarm clock at 4:15 in the morning.

The whistle blew and Ms. Former-Teacher-Turned-Hard-Hat scooted out her chair, dumped her tar back in the thermos, and nodded at me like she'd just done me a great service before returning to her spot on the line. I watched her hurry back, picked up my hard hat, and finished my shift.

The rest of that noisy day, the only things I let myself think about were desks and questions and textbooks. And the next morning, neither my alarm clock nor my dad's knocks could keep me from calling in sick. A few weeks later, I picked up my last paycheck from the Pepsi-Cola Bottling Company. My father wasn't happy that I'd "retired" early from the factory business in the middle of the summer. But I convinced him I'd find another job when I got to college, even if it meant washing pots and pans in the dorm cafeteria. Which it did—I was, after all, experienced in the restaurant business. I didn't mind the dishwashing room where the only sound was the quiet spray of water. It was almost soothing, purposeful even. Each greasy pan, each steel wool, pad reminded me where I was. And where I was going.

Even if there were no jobs waiting for me.

So what are we going to do the rest of our lives? Stay home and watch the parades go by? Amuse ourselves with the glass menagerie, darling? Eternally play those worn-out phonograph records your father left as a painful reminder of him? We won't have a business career—we've given that up because it gave us nervous indigestion! [She laughs wearily.] What

is there left but dependency all our lives? I know so well what becomes of unmarried women who aren't prepared to occupy a position . . . little bird-like women without any nest—eating the crust of humility all their life!
—Amanda, in *The Glass Menagerie* by Tennessee Williams

Light comes slowly through a morning window. You open your eyes, push out the sleep, and stretch your bones. Particles form patterns as the light streams across the room, and your mind follows them. First to the idea of another day, then rapid-fire to the tasks and words, fears and chores that you know will fill it. Like a magnet, the thoughts pull your arms out from under the blankets. You plop your feet over the side of the bed. You sit up. You take one step and then another, slurp some coffee and eat some toast, and before you even know how it happened, you're behind a wheel or a desk or a conveyor belt. The world, it seems, has become aglow in the movement of the morning, and your part—whatever it is— stokes the fire.

It's that "your part" business that gets tricky. Just like marching into a heated debate with cross-examinations like, What were you born for? What are your passions? How can you know what to do? Do you really matter?

Who in the world am I? Ah, that's the great puzzle.

I suppose the questions could appear cliché to anyone who does not wrestle every now and then with his or her lot in life—the one who needs no alarm clock, who shrugs over his routine. To him, such questions are silly, mere distractions even, from meetings or trading, plowing or bottling. To him, time does not afford the luxury of asking. Survival through today's status quo is enough.

This strategy seems cozy, but it's never stuck with me. Many days, I wish it had. I wish I could hand out the same business card I've had all my adult life, like my neighbor who spent forty-eight years as an assistant in the same office. Such consistency must be a certain mercy.

Instead, the questions have been as persistent with me as morning light in a window. What *am* I born for? What gets my blood circulating so fast that I can't wait to get to it? Most times I've hunted for that one single answer each time I picked up a Classified Ads section or sat in a chair for an interview.

But maybe finding this place called vocation is more like waking up each day—when *nothing* seems to happen all at once. First your eyes open to an idea, a little particle of light that you can't stop looking at. You plop your feet on the ground and take one step toward it, and another after it. You slurp up the experience, lick your lips, and before you know it, your whole being is aglow with a mysterious fire inside. Because you've not only been given the tool to poke the flames, to help keep the thing moving, but you've also been warmed by the process as well. At least until you step away from the fire and into the cold.

> *I don't like work—no man does, but I like what is in the work, the chance to find yourself. Your own reality—for yourself, not for others—what no other man can ever know. They can only see the mere show, and never can tell what it really means.*
>
> —Marlow, in *Heart of Darkness* by Joseph Conrad

The hard-hat lady was wrong. Sort of.

Five years after Pepsi, when I graduated—barely—from college (the year was 1981), I hung on to the hope of a career in education, despite the surplus of teachers in the world. My faith was young enough to believe some position would open up in the universe, just for me. And two months after a stoic-looking official handed me my diploma and teaching certificate, my phone rang. A friend knew a friend whose school just created an opening. Did I want an interview? Even if it was only a part-time position teaching remedial English at a "questionable" high school on the other side of Denver?

I was there within an hour. Résumé in hand. The principal looked at me from the other side of experience: gray hair, lines across his forehead, and a softness still in his eyes. He liked my enthusiasm, he said. Besides, the three other applicants were veterans, and he'd have to pay them more. So if I was also willing to coach whatever sport needed an assistant that year, the principal said softly, I could have the job. Who cared that it was girls' basketball and cheerleading—neither of which I had a smidgen of expertise in?

I said yes.

It was a foot in the door of a public school district, and between that part-time salary and waitressing tips from the fine-dining establishment where I worked weekend nights, I could pay for rent, groceries, and car insurance. That first year I earned more money at the restaurant than from the school, which I always found a strange commentary on our culture, but that is another story.

So I dove into my dream and soon rose in the ranks of full-time government employee for the city of Aurora, with benefits I always thought were pretty good, far better than the alternative. I taught remedial English and speech, and coached soccer and debate. (The cheerleading and basketball shtick didn't last long—a good thing for the girls.) For the next five years, I worked as hard as you do in your twenties when you're starting out and wanting to prove something. I graded millions of compositions. I spent long hours with soccer balls and Shakespeare, sophomores, and spelling tests. And I made many, many mistakes that to this day I regret.

Even so, something magical happened whenever a student's eyes traced the ceiling for some rote answer and instead discovered a thrilling question. Whenever another transformed a couple of terrible sentences into meaning that mattered, or found a friend in a book we were reading, or grew from barely able to announce his name into an orator of Martin Luther King Jr. proportions. Yes, despite my limited successes and many failures, the classroom's enchantment did not easily loosen its grip on me. A factory or a drive-in or a dishwashing room was simply no match for the classroom. I mean, who among us cannot still name that teacher or two who first lit the candle of our imagination and sent us in directions we never thought we could go? Those brave souls who gave us permission to wonder, to ask whether there might be something better out there?

Then again, that could be the very reason I spontaneously reached for the Classifieds section of the newspaper one autumn Sunday into my fifth year of teacher status. And why I paused over each education ad a little longer than necessary, allowing my eye to scan other sections—food, government, hospitality, retail—as well. My eye kept wandering for Sundays to come as eventually I left my high school students for graduate school, graduate school for a college teaching position, college teaching for a newspaper, a newspaper for a magazine, and a magazine for a life as—what?—a freelance writer. Full-time. A professional word person.

This last job was hard to explain, especially to those friends who'd ask me to babysit their children during the day because I was at my home and must have had lots of time. It was not a real job, they'd say. I'd sigh. Because it—like passion—was tough to explain.

There are all different kinds of voices calling you to all different kinds of work, and the problem is to find out which is the voice of God rather than of Society, say, or the Superego, or Self-Interest.

By and large a good rule for finding out is this: The kind of work God usually calls you to is the kind of work (a) that you need most to do and (b) that the world most needs to have done. If you really get a kick out of your work, you've presumably met requirement (a), but if your work is writing cigarette ads, the chances are you've missed requirement (b). On the other hand, if your work is being a doctor in a leper colony, you have probably met requirement (b), but if most of the time you're bored and depressed by it, the chances are you have not only bypassed (a), but probably aren't helping your patients much either.

Neither the hair shirt nor the soft berth will do. The place God calls you to is the place where your deep gladness and the world's deep hunger meet.

—Frederick Buechner, *Wishful Thinking*

Sometimes I have felt like Snoopy as he sits atop his doghouse, clanging away on his typewriter, when Charlie Brown comes out to tell him his supper will be a few minutes late. The dog's eyes droop, and he turns back to his machine to type, "Like all writers, I have known great suffering."

The writer's life can indeed be perilous.

By 1994, a few years after my teaching career had officially turned to writing, I received a job offer at a magazine with a national urban focus. This was generally exciting, except that the magazine's office was in another state in another part of the country. Of course, some folks said that Mississippi *was* another country altogether, unlike any other on the planet, but I considered the job offer quite an honor. Two leaders (one African-American, one white) I had long admired not only for their vision of building interracial unity but for their dedication to communicating it in a magazine were asking me to make a three-year commitment, help them "take the magazine to the next level," bring a new sense of vision and editorial direction to their five-year-old publishing venture.

I was amazed by their confidence in my abilities. So in spite of what I knew—or didn't know—about this southern state, I had to wonder if Mississippi might just be a place where the world's deep hunger would meet my new deep gladness: words. Soon I began to realize, though, what such a *meeting* would mean: packing up seven years' worth of memories, friendships, and community I had built in the inner-city neighborhood of Denver where I lived after my suburban teaching career. It meant the probability of losing touch with the neighbor children whom I met when they were in kindergarten and who now were entering junior high school. It meant leaving the only city and state I had ever called home, including my parents and brothers, nephew and nieces, and former colleagues. And of course, it meant leaving a particular way of life, a culture of the West, to enter a completely different one known as Deep South.

It seemed a hard offer, so I flipped through the newspaper ads, just in case. And every night when I went to bed, I tried to imagine myself falling asleep in Mississippi. I tried to get used to the idea of uprooting my life in one city and planting it in another. Even as a single woman who admittedly felt ready—or restless—for new challenges, I agonized over whether I could actually, well, do this.

Still, it was a job possibility like none other. I would be able to cover stories on urban issues, interview church leaders committed to racial reconciliation, provide resources and book reviews for grassroots workers and teachers on the front lines of city life. It was a position that blended everything I cared about: writing, teaching, urban ministry, community, racial justice, and now, publishing. But Mississippi?

I said yes. I found an apartment in West Jackson two miles from the magazine office, and by late May I pulled onto Glen Mary Road to unpack my U-Haul truck, greeted by the editorial team. Together, we carried boxes and suitcases into the little apartment that would be mine.

By mid-June, the city experienced a record-breaking heat wave. Each morning as I arrived at the offices for eight a.m. meetings, temperatures were already into the mid-nineties; it was a heat couched in thick Mississippi humidity, the kind that zaps the life from you the minute you walk outside. I figured this came with the territory, so I did my best to stay near air conditioners, drink a lot of water, and keep focused on the job before me.

There was plenty of work to do. Within a month of starting, I learned the magazine was experiencing financial difficulties. We'd have to be creative to help keep it going for a while. We strategized about several marketing possibilities and collected stories and writers for the next issue. We had long talks about article ideas, editing procedures, networking contacts, advertising support, and, of course, how to advance the work of racial reconciliation through each.

By July, the temperatures soared over one hundred degrees each day, and my bosses asked me to take a pay cut even as we planned new ways to keep the vision of the magazine alive. All the while we kept talking, and all the while the business side of the publication kept struggling.

Finally, in early August, the magazine came out in full color, with thought-provoking articles and helpful information. "A strong issue," if we did say so ourselves. And we did. Readers seemed to agree. I felt good about the stories, the ideas I contributed that generated other, better ideas. From cover to cover, it seemed like a good start for me as its managing editor, and so I kept working hard.

One Friday morning in late August I was working at home, trying desperately to meet our next deadline. Lost in the story on my computer screen, I literally jumped when the phone rang. It was one of my bosses, and he wondered if the three of us could meet. I agreed, and within minutes they were at my door. And nothing in all of creation could have prepared me for the surprise they brought me.

I was being fired. Though they really liked my editing and my writing, it wasn't quite "working out" having me around the office. We saw things differently as far as how to run a magazine, they told me, and so the best thing for everyone was to "let me go"—effective immediately. They appreciated my efforts and admitted that this was one of the hardest parts of their job. Still, it was the right thing to do, and if I wanted to freelance for them in the future, I was welcome to.

Immediately, tears stung my eyes and spilled down my face. Questions exploded inside my head and burst into the already tense room: had I heard right? Had I been in the same office as they had all summer? What in particular wasn't working out? And what about the three-year contract? Or the pay cuts? I uprooted my whole life for *this*?

There were no answers. We sat in silence for what seemed a decade—I, blubbering like an unprofessional idiot; they, staring at their shoes. Finally, they rose to leave, and when I shut the door behind them, I screamed and paced and cursed and paced some more, circling the chair and the couch in my tiny living room. What would I do now? Who would hire me after being such a failure at a magazine I had believed in so much?

What *was* I supposed to do with my life? More questions pounded in my head, like the headache I was getting. I blew my nose so much that afternoon and cried so long I didn't think I had much left in me.

The phone rang. This time it was my friend Clarence, an African-American pastor who was in town for a conference. He had already heard about my sudden shift in employment status—news travels fast in the South—and wanted to know how I was feeling. I blubbered again. Then he demanded I meet him at a coffee shop where we could talk and pray. I obeyed.

That was the beginning of the healing. Clarence let me rant and rave about the woes of my great suffering as he sipped his coffee and nodded his head. How could I have been fired from a job that meant so much to me? Where would I go now?

Oh, I moaned and suffered like one who had no hope. This wasn't fair. I felt as if war had just broken out in my homeland. Or that someone had just robbed my favorite uncle. Or that my twin sister—if I had one—had just been diagnosed with some debilitating disease. I would never understand what I was supposed to do with my life.

Certainly, losing a job does indeed feel devastatingly close to the end of the world at the time that it is taken from you. Especially when you have wandered so long to find it.

But of course, it is not the end of the world. Or even the end of a town or city. Yes, the injustice is painful; the confusion is exhausting. And sometimes even Christian leaders get it wrong, really wrong, Clarence was saying to me. The reality, he whispered across his mug, was that this did *not* come as a shock to the Maker of the universe. I wiped my nose and swallowed my cold coffee.

Then the pastor continued to pastor: "You know what? The One who led you to Mississippi in the first place won't stop taking care of you. Isn't it great that your confidence and security don't come from what you do in your career? They're rooted in the work of Christ, the Risen One!" That truth, Clarence said, would get me through the next few difficult months.

His kindness, along with the letters, phone calls, and prayers of a community of faithful friends from across the country, cushioned me from feeling like a total loser during the next few months of adjusting—again—to life in Mississippi. Their support shielded me—I believe now—from being eaten alive by the toxic bitterness I felt toward my former bosses. Few let me whine for long before they asked what new freelancing project I was working on or what trip I was planning in the southern states.

Their words were balm to my career wounds. So much so that by the end of that year, I knew I had stayed long enough in Mississippi and since—as you know—I'd long been in love with New York City, I found the courage, bolstered by also locating a roommate in Manhattan, to pack up another U-Haul truck. The next February I drove across country to start over. One more time.

I have come to refer to my time in Mississippi as "The Great Canning," the place where I got the boot—canned, fired, let go, terminated, dismissed. Whatever we want to call it. It was the place where I learned career is more about community than it is benefits, just as vocation is more about vulnerability than it is vision.

The journey of discovering what we're born for seems first to lead us to death. That is not a hopeless place, though. I suspect from it will emerge some clue about what—or whom—we'd be willing to die for. For from the cold stone of a threatened life we instinctively venture back to the fire, the one that warms us and keeps our blood moving.

Your work is to keep cranking the flywheel that turns the gears that spin the belt in the engine of belief that keeps you and your desk in midair.
—Annie Dillard, *The Writing Life*

And so I write. And I teach—as a college professor; that's the fancy term for working with words *and* young people. After reading about it in another online classified ad, I asked about this job at another college in another state. In Massachusetts, just north of Boston near the water. They were kind and offered it to me. And it was not hard to say yes. Because here I am teaching writing while I write. Writing while I teach.

I suppose I have finally discovered: writing feeds my soul. Teaching flavors the food. Most days at least.

Both, I also know, are privileges and passions, the products of a single step on a road that became an expedition that turned into a life. Orchestrated, it's easy to see from here, by Someone far more savvy than any Monster Jobs employment service. How else could it be that my office was even next door to the art professors' offices and studios in the art building on campus? Every day I saw paintings and drawings and sculptures in progress, an astonishingly gracious rotation for these roaming eyes.

And every now and then, people tell me I have a real job—one with a business card I hope to hand out for some years to come. It has not come without its bumps and wrong turns along the way, revealing to me the secret I have known since I left Mississippi: work that is also vocation has more to do with the gift of living than the earning of it.

Yet, it is a freedom, I think, we can know only if—or when—we stop our industrious madness long enough to step toward the embers. For there, in that reflective pause, is also the breath of life, the place where the question of purpose no longer steals our joy but invites it.

And though this pause before life's fire is truer than any newspaper ad or career dream ever will be, I have to admit, even now, I still pick up the Classifieds. Just in case.

*Life is not orderly. No matter how we
try to make life so, right in the middle
of it we die, lose a leg, fall in love,
drop a jar of applesauce.*
—Natalie Goldberg,
Wild Mind: Living the Writer's Life

ro·mance (rō-māns´, rō´māns´) [Middle
English, from Old French romans, *romance,
work written in French*, from Vulgar Latin
*romanice (scribere), *(to write) in the vernac-
ular*, from Latin Romanicus, *Roman*, from
Romanus; see Roman.] noun.

A love affair.

**Ardent emotional attachment or involve-
ment between people; love.**

A strong, sometimes short-lived attachment,
fascination, or enthusiasm for something.

A mysterious or fascinating quality or
appeal, as of something adventurous, heroic,
or strangely beautiful.

FOUR

Hungry Heart

and the romances I never knew

How odd that sex should be so simple and love such a complication.
—P. D. James, *The Lighthouse*

I am in the emergency room of the local hospital in our New England town. Early this wintry morning, I have driven my husband here because he is in such pain he cannot sleep. We didn't know where to go because we are only a few months settled into this town. This new job at the college brought us here, so we haven't yet noticed where the hospitals are.

Why would we need one?

But this morning, my husband feels like someone kicked him so hard in the ribs that he cannot move without struggling for a breath. He cannot lie down because of the throbs and jabs in his back. His face is pale and his eyes scared. So I look up the hospital on MapQuest, grab my car keys, and hurry to this emergency entrance. A kind doctor looks at my husband's ribs and tells him he shouldn't feel like this if, in fact, no one has kicked him, or if there has been no recent trauma to his body. There hasn't been, we tell him.

The doctor frowns. Immediately he sends my husband down the hall for X-rays of his chest. When he comes back, the doctor reports there is fluid on his lungs. Now the doctor is sending him down another hall for a CAT scan—one of those technological miracles I don't understand that somehow can see underneath skin and bones. None of this has taken away the fear from my husband's eyes, though he tries not to show me as they wheel him away.

I stand at the end of the hall until I can no longer see him. I turn around, looking again at where I last watched him, uncertain what to do next. Someone points me to the emergency room waiting area and that seems like a good idea. A young mother sits in a corner, a professional football game playing quietly on a television set above her. Worry lines her face. A gray-haired woman sits across from her, a tissue pressed against her eyes. And a couple cling to each other as they follow a nurse into a room.

I glance at the television, but I don't care about touchdowns and interceptions right now. Maybe some hotshot administrator believes the game will remind emergency visitors like me of the normal things in life. Maybe television will divert our attention for a little while, calm us down, help us cope as we watch life still going on. Look there: athletes are still playing games in chilly stadiums and television stations are still airing them. People in living rooms somewhere are relaxing on couches watching and cheering and doing the things you do when you gather around a televised event.

I am not one of them. It isn't working for me. The minute I walk into this room, normalcy leaves. Ordinary is a long time ago. It feels far from here, from how life plays out in the everyday when wives throw chicken and onions into pans and neighbors shovel snow and husbands do not feel like their ribs have been broken for no reason at all. No, in this room, the possibility of loss weighs heavy on your shoulders. Football looks ridiculous. Normal now seems a luxury.

Love makes it so.

If you care even an ounce for another human being, rest assured your heart will be wrecked if his living, breathing body suddenly needs a room marked by emergencies. (It will be wrecked, that is, if you too are living and breathing.) And when you marry the love of your life, when you vow your presence to him for each day and each month of each year hereafter, the last thing you expect is to sit in a hospital's emergency room, wondering why a television set is on when all you want to know is when you will see your husband again. It is a moment a million miles from the romance that first took you to the altar, but of course, it is no less passionate.

This, though, wrings out your core.

Oh, life is a glorious cycle of song,
A medley of extemporanea;
And love is a thing that can never go wrong;
And I am Marie of Roumania.

—Dorothy Parker

Most of my adult life I thought marriage was what other people did. It was a nice thing for them, charming and necessary and important even. I was happy when my friends did it, and I'd even buy them crystal wineglasses or candlesticks when I could afford them. I'd go to their weddings and get teary during the vows; I'd ask for seconds at the reception dinner and engage in meaningful conversations at the table when the band struck up a dance song. I could celebrate the decisions of others with the best of them.

But marriage—that messy lifelong commitment-to-intimacy thing— was not a vision that landed often in my head, not an idea that lingered more than a few minutes before I'd sweep it out and replace it with something, well, real. I suppose I'd spent too many years building a shield around my soul to protect me from the bizarre concept of wife and husband. It was a sturdy stone wall, not easily accessed, each section constructed by a convenient excuse, a busy schedule, or a spiritual insight.

And why not? My single life was full of adventurous trips; my vocational options, constantly challenging; and my art, ministry, and friendships, rich and fulfilling. As dreadful as it might sound to those infatuated with the fairy-tale bridal industry, I really was content as an unmarried woman. I was happy with the lifestyle I'd been given. Why would I spoil it by flirting with romance?

Singleness was familiar. Simple. It was safe medicine, much easier to swallow than dating and flowers and hormones. So when I thought of marriage, it was not something I expected to need.

After all, the stone wall had taken time to build.

It began forming early on in my suburban home as I watched my parents struggle to put together something no one had taught them how to do. Their marriage was a result of a weekend leave in 1953 when both were serving in the Air Force. Away from active duty, my mother chatted at a party with a skinny dark-haired man who impressed her enough that two weeks later, she agreed to marry him. Only problem was that they were stationed at different military bases in different states. Two months later they planned a rendezvous in Reno, Nevada, honeymooned for the weekend, and returned to their separate units until they could complete the military transfers to live together as husband and wife.

Two years later my oldest brother was born. Soon another brother and then me—but you already know that story. With three children in three years in the 1950s also came a suburban existence dripping with duty and determination. My mom and pop did all the things middle-class American parents did then: they cooked us big Sunday breakfasts, filled our stockings at Christmas, and gave us chores to teach us responsibility. They drove my brothers and me to camps and lessons and Little League, just like they were supposed to do. They baked and corrected, vacationed and clothed, making ours a safe and generous childhood. Certainly, we were—and are—the better for it.

But I'm not sure they were. In fact, their wordless romance left a giant question mark on my brothers and me. We had plenty to eat and wear and keep us busy but not much conversation about how to relate to others. So when this strange new world called love and the opposite sex came upon us, we floundered often and anxiously on our own.

As we grew up, so did our curiosity, and I wondered whether our parents loved each other like TV couples did, like Rob and Laura on *The Dick Van Dyke Show*. Did my dad show my mom the same kind of smitten romance we saw in the heroes on the *Wild Wild West* or *Bonanza*? Did our parents feel utterly lost or crushed without the other? Did they hold hands when we weren't looking?

I was twelve years old when I stole my first peek at what I came to perceive as husband-and-wife matters. On a summer afternoon when my dad was at work, my mom at the tennis club, and my brothers who knows where—they were teenagers by this time—I wandered into my parents' bedroom. It was across the hall from mine, next to the common bathroom and diagonal from the spare room my dad used as a den. I don't know why I was alone that day, though I don't remember it being particularly unusual. With older brothers and not many girls in the neighborhood, I spent a lot of time on my own. This one afternoon I went looking for something to relieve my boredom. And my loneliness.

What I found was not what I expected.

The Colorado sun fell through their window, casting alluring rays across the bed. I followed them and saw the light drawing odd sparkles across a pile of glossy magazine covers beside my father's nightstand. Little particles of dust floated in the light, but that isn't what I noticed most.

Instinctively I reached for the top magazine and flipped. It was a business journal full of big words and dull ads. I was about to toss it back on the pile, when the magazine beneath it suddenly caught my eye. I picked it up. I turned page after page, and though I didn't understand what I saw, I couldn't put it down. I turned it this way and that, and felt a taste of something completely unfamiliar the back of my throat. Page after page was both a puzzle and a fascination until finally I flipped one page and another long picture dropped out in the center.

I had never seen a woman's body look like this before. Oh, I had been in the locker room at school for gym class, even at the local swimming pool where older women changed into their bathing suits, but I'd never noticed anything like this. My palms felt strange. My head felt achy.

And some small bricklike matter began to form around my twelve-year-old female heart. The magazine from my dad's nightstand, with its strange pictures, cast a peculiar and uncomfortable spell.

The sunlight outside the window had faded when I heard the front door open. I tossed the magazine back beneath the *BusinessWeek* and straightened the pile in a hurry—certain I'd been doing something I wasn't supposed to be doing. My mom hollered from the kitchen to come help with dinner, and I punched the dust from the air to hide any evidence of my delinquency.

My cheeks felt hot with shame and I didn't like it. My mom yelled again from the kitchen, but I rushed into the bathroom, washed my hands and face, and rubbed them hard on a towel. As I did, I caught a sight in the mirror that made me feel embarrassed, ugly, ridiculous.

I was like them. Not yet a teenager, no longer a child, I was nonetheless a *girl*, which meant I'd also someday be a woman who men might look at in funny ways. The realization dropped in my stomach like the flu.

I ran down the hall to the safety of the kitchen, grabbed knives, spoons, and forks and began to set the table. My mother moved between the counter and the stove; still dressed in her tennis skirt and sleeveless blouse, her skin smooth and tan from the sun. Did she know about that magazine? Did she get those same confusing feelings about those pictures? Were men supposed to look at women like that? Did she expect it from my dad?

Everything in me wanted to ask her. She was stirring the tuna casserole, and my brothers and my dad hadn't yet come home. So I could have. The moment was right. We weren't talking about anything else.

But I never found the courage to ask the questions. She didn't ask what I'd been doing, so I just poured the milk. We finished our supper in our ordinary kitchen, passed the vegetables, and sat in our usual silence around the table, connected by blood and a name and an awkward love.

I didn't look up from my plate that night.

I spent the next many years afraid of the answers to the questions I never asked my mom.

And what's romance? Usually, a nice little tale where you have everything As You Like It, where rain never wets your jacket and gnats never bite your nose, and it's always daisy-time.
  —D. H. Lawrence, *Studies in Classic American Literature*

They are looking at my husband's body while he lies still on his back in the center of a huge metal doughnut. The contraption moves around him, clicking and zooming from each angle. The lights are bright; the room is plain. He struggles for short breaths while the CAT scan rotates over his torso—clicking, zooming, and monitoring some more as it moves.

My husband tells me this story once he is wheeled back into what they call a transition room. His voice is quiet, emotionless in the telling, not at all what it usually is. He tries to lie still. I listen as I watch a nurse insert a needle into his arm; it is connected to a plastic bag that drips clear liquid. This, she says, will relieve his pain. She smiles awkwardly as she tells us she does not think he will go home tonight. The CAT scan has confirmed what we have imagined but would never say: his life is fragile right now. He is suddenly dependent on more than an exercise routine and organic foods to sustain him. He needs medical intervention. And mercy.

I scoot my chair in close to him, because that is all I can think to do, though I don't really know what to say to him. He shuts his eyes, his face still pale from the pain.

Usually his face is tan. Rugged and handsome. He is used to being outside, walking the beach or kayaking the waves or sailing a small boat in the ocean. These are typical adventures for him, the daily encounters with the sea that he loves near the home that we share. He grew up on these encounters in his native land of Australia, and I know he is more alive when he is outdoors. When he is on the water in the sun, feeling the wind on his cheeks, tasting the salt in the air, new life drops into his soul, and he comes back whistling. He looks better out there, much better, where he is more familiar with sails and masts than IV needles and transition rooms in hospitals.

How could he be here? His arms are strong, his energy high, his shoulders and legs and hands firm and sturdy. I know: I have walked many blocks in New York City beside him, roamed cobblestone paths in Prague next to him, and ridden a bike behind him along the Jersey Shore. In the waves off Australia's Sunshine Coast, I have held on to his shoulders when I felt afraid and he was not. And I have twirled beneath his arms when we have tried to salsa, laughing with each step, hoping some day to succeed.

This place, though, does not prove any of that. Here, none of his adventures or passions or dances matter. Here, tests and monitors and syringes are the norm.

The kind doctor pushes open the door gently, and his eyes are serious. He tells us they have found the cause of the pain: two pulmonary embolisms are in my husband's right lung; they could move at any minute and cause a stroke. Or worse.

The doctor will begin immediately to thin his blood and start the official paperwork to admit him. He will order more tests and watch him carefully around the clock. My husband must stay in the hospital, the doctor says again, and that is when it hits me: he will not be next to me tonight in bed.

I grab his hand; his skin is warm, familiar. I cannot imagine it any other way.

There is no safe investment. To love at all is to be vulnerable. Love anything, and your heart will certainly be wrung and possibly be broken. If you want to make sure of keeping it intact, you must give your heart to no one, not even to an animal. Wrap it carefully round with hobbies and little luxuries; avoid all entanglements; lock it up safe in the casket or coffin of your selfishness. But in that casket—safe, dark, motionless, airless—it will change. It will not be broken; it will become unbreakable, impenetrable, irredeemable. The alternative to tragedy, or at least to the risk of tragedy, is damnation. The only place outside Heaven where you can be perfectly safe from all the dangers and perturbations of love is Hell.

—C. S. Lewis, *The Four Loves*

My initial education in what men expected of women was easily reinforced when I entered my teen years. Each time I walked out the door, the lesson would greet me. We'd visit a family friend across town—an older bachelor who was a painter—and find his apartment cluttered with stacks of magazines featuring naked women on the covers. (My brothers never did complain about those visits.) We'd drive a few hours to visit relatives and observe scores of billboards along the way with women in slinky bikinis selling lotion or beer. Even when we went to the Denver Broncos football games, we'd see cheerleaders on the sidelines wearing tiny skirts and tinier tops.

From television commercials, movies, and ads to my brothers and friends, I kept learning the same thing. That message was this: a woman was her body. And her body was an object for amusement. A symbol for entertainment. A shape for one purpose.

Nothing else.

I didn't see much to contradict this or hear many other definitions, so I assumed for a long time that this was the common currency between men and women. The roles were clear, the hierarchy clearer. No matter if your soul was born wanting more than images and objects, yearning to be more than a picture, this was simply how the world—or at least Colorado—turned. So much so that, eventually, sex and intimacy, lust and connection, all began to mean the same thing. Each morphed into the other. There were no distinctions.

And it felt overwhelming. So I'd plop another stone on the wall around my being. Whenever my family went back to our bachelor friend's apartment, I'd bury my nose into whatever novel I'd brought along. On trips in the car, I'd focus on the landscape instead of the billboards. And at the football games, well, I learned about first downs, fumbles, and field goals. The more I understood the game, I reasoned, the more I would belong to those in charge and the further away I would be from the tiny skirts and pompoms.

Yes, I was a female. A girl. A woman in the making. But I did not have to act like one. Instead, I'd tackle the ski slopes or the soccer fields, feeling more at home with coaches and athletes than I did with crushes and boyfriends. In sports, at least I knew what I was supposed to do, even if I wasn't great at it. With high school boys, the questions just loomed like a scoreboard at the beginning of a game. I went to the homecoming dance with the brother of a friend, and to the prom with a boy a year younger, but they were *nice little tales*, awkward romances, short-lived and insignificant, much like my athletic career.

Yet these tales honed my survival skills and carried over into my twenties. I'd jog or hike, write or read, teach or coach, travel or explore so much of the world that I wouldn't have time to think about this awkward tension between men and women, let alone enter it for more than a few months. And I'd be so miserably happy and exhausted that I wouldn't even notice I was alone. I had friendships. I had community.

I even had Jesus, who—according to the older ladies in church—was the ultimate husband, the Bridegroom of all bridegrooms. I'd roll my eyes each time they'd say it. For though the title was certainly true (albeit a corny romanticizing of the love behind all loves), the good Lord did not mean the same to me as he did to them. I did not need—or want—Jesus as my husband. I needed his friendship.

And he gave it.

Even so, because gender roles confounded me, I'd use my new spiritual language to avoid men. I had an arsenal of religious reasons—"it's just not God's will"—for each no when Curt kept calling for dates in college. My language became more pious once I graduated and started my teaching career, especially when Mark persisted with invitations to movies or parties. And though Curt was a nice enough guy and Mark an interesting man, my early education about men had not yet been converted as my soul had. The survival skills merely changed. Now, instead of soccer fields or ski slopes, I'd escape each interaction with piety or scripture. I'd drop lofty euphemisms into each conversation and emotional distance into every sigh. Better not to get distracted from eternal matters. Better not to be an object.

Better to avoid all entanglements and lock up the heart in a casket.

Place me like a seal over your heart,
like a seal on your arm;
for love is as strong as death,
its jealousy unyielding as the grave.
It burns like a blazing fire.

—Song of Songs 8:6

Then there was Timothy. A beautifully gentle twenty-six-year-old man of Italian ancestry, he sat beside me in a communication class during graduate school in Virginia. I was twenty-eight, straight out of public school teaching, and interested only in advancing my career. Timothy walked with me across campus one day, all the way to the library, though he didn't need any books. I, however, needed to bury myself in a study carrel, monastic-like, to ensure my academic success. He stood that afternoon at the entrance to the library, tall and tanned in the fall sun, fiddling with his backpack, staring at his feet, until finally I had to go inside to study. I reached for the door.

"Could we have dinner?" he asked. I paused and glanced up into his face. His eyes were goofy—there's no other word for it—as he smiled. Hopeful. Sincere. Tender.

He was not looking at me the way I'd expected. This was a look I could not define.

"Um, I have to study," I coughed. He nodded. But the next day after class, he asked again. And the day after that. And the day after that. Finally, one night we were sitting across from each other over soup at a local diner. He talked for a long time about his family, his parents, and his childhood, smiling and beaming with each detail. He dreamed aloud about going overseas, wanting to work as a missionary, studying the language, hoping God would someday allow him to fulfill his dream.

With a wife.

I asked the waitress for more water. Timothy backed up. The last thing he wanted, he said softly, his brown eyes diffusing, was for me to feel pressure. Some things only God could know, he said. Some things might never make sense.

He was right about that.

So I told him about skiing in Colorado, teaching sophomore English, and coaching debate and junior varsity girls' basketball. He asked about my family, and I relayed a few uncomfortable memories. He wanted to know my dreams, and I tried my best to concoct some. The words were becoming untangled.

Timothy spent the rest of our graduate school days walking me across campus, opening doors for me, and taking me to dinner or coffee. He'd plunk down his backpack on a desk beside mine in the library and study hard, waiting patiently for me each night when the library would close. In those seven or so months we were together, the kindness of his spirit never waned, and the goofy look in his eyes never faded, especially when he'd tell me how beautiful he thought I was.

"Inside and out," he'd say, his hand on his heart. "God made you so," he'd add with a glimmer. I'd shrug, look away, and wonder about missionary life. And in between exams and papers, jogs and study groups, I'd ask Jesus, my friend, for help, any help at all, in understanding this strange and beautiful man who sat beside me in communications class, looking at me like I mattered.

When the year ended, I told Timothy I was sorry. I could not see myself living or working overseas. It was a grand vision, a noble and important mission, but it was not mine. It was his. He, of course, should pursue it, I whispered. For God's sake. When he listened to me, he nodded. He could not keep from hugging me anyway. And so dear Timothy flew across the world, I returned to Colorado, and the education I thought I'd come to gain really meant another one had started to die.

Because at least to one man, I knew I was not an object.

"My head is quite empty," answered the Woodman; *"but once I had brains and a heart also; so, having tried them both, I should much rather have a heart."*

—Tin Woodman, in *The Wonderful Wizard of Oz* by Frank Baum

They are doing an ultrasound on various parts of my husband's body, looking magically (again) for the clot that sent the fragments to his lung. It is the second day that he has been in the hospital, away from our living room and kitchen, from the bedroom where his clothes and books and shoes wait for him.

A technician is sitting behind a computer screen in a small dark room no bigger than our bathroom. He is pressing a gadget against my husband's greasy leg, talking with each movement and staring closely at a shadowy image on the screen. He studies the lines and colors and talks some more. My husband breathes deeply and shivers.

Then the technician—who is a new employee at the hospital, I learn later—suddenly becomes quiet. He's spotted a spot, a black blob in the calf of the left leg. He thinks this is the source of the excruciating crisis, and he seems thrilled about showing the doctors what he has found, if for nothing else than to confirm that they have hired the right man for this job. He angles the screen to show my husband, pointing to the spot the way an obstetrician would show a baby to an expectant mother.

It is all very weird.

But my husband's doctor is pleased to trace the progress, he tells us on his morning rounds. This is a good sign because now they can monitor it specifically. The body, he says, will eventually and naturally wrap scar tissue around the clot to keep it from breaking off and shooting through parts of his body where they do not belong. Until then, my husband should not move much from this hospital bed. From this sterile room where no pictures hang on the wall.

I study my husband's face and find it's a blend of relief and worry. He listens to the doctor, but we both know he does not belong here. At home, though, there are no monitors or IVs; at home, his life would be in danger.

We are not ready for that. And so we wait, together, he in a paisley hospital gown, I in my winter sweater and jeans, all the more aware that this moment, this now, is one more gift of the many we have already received.

I suppose we learn a little more about love each time it is threatened.

I think that God doesn't necessarily want us to be happy. He wants us to be lovable. Worthy of love. Able to be loved by Him. We don't start off being all that lovable, if we're honest. What makes people hard to love? Isn't it what is commonly called selfishness?

—William Nicholson, *Shadowlands*

Five years after Timothy flew overseas, I'd entered an engagement—and then a breakup or meltdown, depending on your perspective—with a man who tried hard to convince me that the early lessons I'd learned about women and men were true. It was a frightful encounter that left me looking again for the stone wall. Or the casket. Either was a better option than marriage, but that is a story I have already let go of, in a journey and a tale that I've come to believe is the other side of passion: fear. (For more on this, see my book *fear: a spiritual navigation* [Harold Shaw Publishers, 2001].)

By the summer I turned thirty-eight years old, I was far from that fearful place, literally, and working as a writer in Manhattan. I was enamored with the charm and life of the city where poets recited love songs in the subways and tourists watched love stories on Broadway. From the Italian restaurants and the Central Park carriages to the street fairs and bridges across the rivers, this city spelled romance at every turn.

For those who thought they needed it.

I'd joined a Presbyterian church in Manhattan whose congregation was 70 percent single, and though I hardly found myself identifying with the crowd at coffee hour who hoped to "meet prospective dates," I felt at home in the rich diversity of possibilities. I felt stirred by the arts and stimulated by discussions. I was in love with the adventure that happened every time I left my apartment and absorbed by the talent and theology of the people I'd meet.

New York is a great antidote for all kinds of aches.

While friends spoke daily about their desires for marriage, I never quite understood what the big deal was. I had witnessed only a handful of attractive marriages that had survived difficult circumstances; dozens more—including my parents'—had ended with separation or divorce. Marriage was not exactly a picture of eternal bliss in my mind. When I lived in a city where the entire world passed me on a single day, marriage really was the last thing I had to think about.

I certainly did not expect anything but a few published articles when a friend and I booked a flight to England and confirmed our registration at an international Christian reconciliation conference there. A few editors I knew were interested in covering the five-day seminar if I could provide photos along with stories, so in typical freelancing form, I planned a trip abroad for the sake of traveling and hoped my writing would cover the costs.

Once I had scribbled and interviewed enough during each day at the conference, my friend and I would hire a car and drive to Oxford or Cambridge. The cobblestone roads and towering cathedrals of these ancient towns reminded me of the fairy tales I read as a girl, of courageous knights, magical castles, and ladies with long golden hair. The architecture demanded my awe, and the gardens stole my senses. England was an enchanting land, teeming with history, romance, and imagination. After each adventure, we'd return to the conference, and I'd make the transition from play to work.

I don't know if I remembered needing photos before I noticed the stocky, blue-eyed photographer or after seeing him. I watched him clicking and zooming up and down the aisles, maneuvering interesting photo angles. I knew when I saw him that it might be beneficial to approach him—on a professional basis, of course—to fulfill my journalistic obligations. What did it matter that I also noticed his handsome, rugged, artistic face? All I needed were photos.

I walked up to him, introduced myself, and asked about getting a few of his pictures for the magazines I was working for. He stopped what he was doing, turned slowly toward me, and answered me in a low Australian accent. I cleared my throat, then glanced away toward the crowd that was breaking for the evening. I knew he had just said something in English, but I couldn't make out the words. I think it was something about being glad to help.

"And Chris. My name is Chris," he said, waving as we walked out of the cathedral.

A few nights later Chris asked if I'd join him and one of his "mates" at a local pub. We wandered around the corner and into a conversation that lasted several hours. Over fish and chips we talked about literature and writing, justice and reconciliation, faith and cultures. He too had worked as a writer. And he too found himself traveling a lot, working with youth in high schools, and challenging church communities throughout his country. His passion was inviting, his creativity engaging.

The more we talked, though, the more I noticed something familiar forming in his eyes. There was no mistaking the look—and no other word to describe it—goofy. I knew I was in trouble, but I reasoned he lived on the other side of the world. I was safe.

When the conference ended, Chris promised to send photos as soon as they were developed. My friend and I extended him and his mates a polite invitation to "stop by the next time you're in New York." England was enchanting, but it was time to go back to reality. I was certain I was safe, as certain as I had been teaching and writing and reminding my single friends that you didn't have to be married to be content.

Within a few weeks of being back in New York, the phone rang. It was the Aussie wanting to know if it would be all right with me if he booked a flight from England (before returning Down Under) to come visit. I held the receiver away from me for an instant, wondering if I had heard him right. I didn't know how to answer him, so he assumed that was a yes. I hung up, amazed and terrified that Chris had called at all.

I was nervous when I picked him up from the airport, but I reminded myself this was only temporary; the man had never been to New York City before, and it was just a short sightseeing visit. Harmless enough. Easy to do. A nice gesture of hospitality. No big deal.

But within the first twenty-four hours, Chris sat on the couch in my living room and felt compelled to tell me more of his life story. He had been thinking of moving on from his mission agency; he was interested in writing more. I wondered where he was going with this, why I needed this information about him.

Then he told me he had been married before. He might as well have pulled out a grenade and tossed it into the living room. Yes, he was in his forties, and I was in my late thirties, and the odds of ever meeting someone these days at this age who had *not* been married were slim. That was thoughtful of him, wasn't it? He wanted to put it out there for me so I wouldn't have any question about him, so I could know from day one that he'd be honest with me. It wasn't as if we were planning our lives together or anything. We did meet only a few weeks before.

I tried to get it clear in my head. Being married before meant that he was now divorced, right? Right, he said softly, regretting even having to make such an admission. Somewhere out there in the world was an ex-wife, right? Right, he whispered again. It ended several years ago when she woke up one morning and decided it'd be best if he left. They'd been husband and wife only a few years, but something went amiss for her, and she did not want him around. No matter what he said or did, she was not changing her mind. So he packed his suitcases, grabbed his books and camera, and left. He'd call every so often to see if she would reconcile, but she was not interested. And that was it, a crushing blow to him, though now, in my apartment, he confessed that the marriage was a mistake in the first place. In retrospect, he should not have gone to the altar with her at all.

In retrospect?! This was too much to hear so early. I tried to change the subject to films, trips, books—anything that would take me away from the truth he had just divulged and into something more frivolous or shallow. I wasn't sure what to do with his admission, but one thing was clear: I knew this was a man who'd go below the surface.

His two-week stay turned into ten, and I shocked my family (and myself) by bringing Chris home for Thanksgiving. He had never experienced an American Thanksgiving, and my family had never seen me bring a man home for a holiday. When Chris asked for seconds on turkey and stuffing and they told him stories of growing up, I wondered if my days were numbered.

But the Aussie flew home, spent Christmas with his family, packed his bags, and moved back to New York, landing a part-time job at the Presbyterian church I attended and an apartment above mine. He dove into his new life like an artist at his canvas: serious, focused, and passionate. He made no secret that he was pursuing a relationship with me, that he was "intrigued" by my character and "fascinated" by my lifestyle. He told me he had not met many women like me who were both "strong in faith and sensitive in nature." I rolled my eyes, blushing at his affirmations, and just as quickly challenging his appraisals—after all, he had known me only six months. Time would tell, I told him.

I waited. But he did not go anywhere. Instead, one Friday night as we walked across the Brooklyn Bridge, the goofy look surfaced. He stopped halfway across, turned to me, and asked me to marry him.

Instead of fireworks over the bay like you see in the movies, a hurricane blew through my soul, stirring up painful residue and debris from my past education. The tangled words flew out of my mouth and onto his well-meaning intentions. We argued and disputed every possible reason why we should or should not be together. And when I finally ended the discussion that night with no commitment one way or another, he retreated into three months of distance.

And waited.

Daughters of Jerusalem, I charge you
    by the gazelles and by the does of the field:
Do not arouse or awaken love until it so desires.

Listen! My lover!
    Look! Here he comes,
leaping across the mountains,
    bounding over the hills.
My lover is like a gazelle or a young stag.
    Look! There he stands behind our wall,
gazing through the windows,
    peering through the lattice.

My lover spoke and said to me, "Arise, my darling,
my beautiful one, and come with me."

—Song of Songs, 2:7-10

Chris is waiting to come home.

Six long days in the hospital has meant the memories of our life together—photos and stories and adventures with each other—have been my companion this week. They've kept me company. I remember the Brooklyn Bridge strolls and Central Park bike rides, the arguments and challenges, the hugs and the hormones flying. I remember walking down Ninety-fifth Street and peering into the future only to realize I could not imagine it without this man. I remember trying desperately to understand God's view on romance, marriage, divorce; poring over scripture; talking with friends wiser than I, remembering other relationships and marriages and divorces; and finally giving up on anything but redemption.

I remember my lover's face at the altar, goofy with joy, and then patient those first years when we learned to live together with everyday quirks and demands, when he brought fresh flowers home every few weeks. But more recently, I remember his nose and cheeks last Sunday morning pale from pain. I am glad to gaze upon his face now, color still not what it was but stunning nonetheless, in the best of ways.

Alive. In love. Still.

And how can I not remember the time I woke up one morning in our little Harlem apartment, a few years after we had said our vows? My hair wasn't brushed, my eyes were puffy with sleep, and my face as natural as it came. I wore an old T-shirt and tried to wake up. Chris set a cup of coffee on the bedside table—as he did each morning—and he looked. At me.

"What?" I muttered.

"You're beautiful," he whispered, moving romance to a whole new level.

"Right. I'm lookin' real good right now," I diverted, gulping caffeine. Without skipping a beat, my husband took my hand and said simply, "What's that got to do with beauty?"

I shake my head in awe. For this man from the other side of the world—divorced and broken and passionate—has made me believe in romance and love. And marriage.

Even if it is the hardest thing I've ever done, it is by far the most amazing.

Chris taps me on the shoulder. It's freezing outside. I help him with his coat as he moves from the wheelchair into the car. He is healthier than he was a week ago, though hardly back to normal. He is, however, well enough for the doctor to release him from the hospital; he can come home where he belongs. To sleep in our bed. To stand in our shower. To listen to the rhythm of our lives together, the hum of the refrigerator, the whir of the heater, the ring of the phone, the pull of our hearts to each other.

We turn into the driveway, and the porch sparkles more than when it was first built. I lean over and kiss my husband. Hard. And I know for a moment that even this, a love so rich and full and intimate, is only a portion of what is to come.

Tomorrow, of course, we will argue. He will leave his shoes where they don't belong, and I will complain when he does. We will talk and not listen, struggle to communicate through loaded language, and huddle in close to each other when we are afraid.

Marriage, after all, like romance and relationships, is prickly stuff. Love is a mystery that can't be solved or reduced to neat formulas or strategies, no matter how many clues we find along the way.

I like living. I have sometimes been wildly despairing, acutely miserable, racked with sorrow, but through it all I still know quite certainly that just to be alive is a grand thing.
—Agatha Christie,
An Autobiography

---

suffer \Suf'fer\, v. t. [imp. & p. p. Suffered; p. pr. & vb. n. Suffering.] [OE. suffren, soffren, OF. sufrir, sofrir, F. souffrir, (assumed) LL. sofferire, for L. sufferre; sub under + ferre to bear, akin to E. bear. See Bear to support.]

To feel, or endure, with pain, annoyance, etc.; to submit to with distress or grief; to undergo; as, to suffer pain of body, or grief of mind.

To endure or undergo without sinking; to support; to sustain; to bear up under.

noun: a state of prolonged anguish and privation: misery, woe, wretchedness.

FIVE

Suffering Souls

and the secrets I've yet to learn

Lips that taste of tears, they say,
Are the best for kissing.
—Dorothy Parker, "Threnody"

I see now there was a reason Chris came home from the hospital.

His nerve endings worked that early morning, sending a message to his brain that must have sounded something like, "Mayday! Mayday! Something's not right down here!" Which pushed him off the couch, hurried me behind the wheel of our car, and brought the emergency room doctor into our lives. Pain sent him to a place where he could get help. If it hadn't been for that, the doctor said, we'd have sent my husband somewhere else.

And we weren't exactly ready for that.

Being near *that place* has a way of helping you look at life.

Still, this state of acute anguish of suffering wasn't something I'd naturally sign up for. Uninvited, it sits like an elephant in the living room, munching on straw, big loopy tears sliding down its trunk. I'd rather pretend it isn't there, but there it sits. And truth be told, we can't walk through marriage or love, jobs or adventures, paintings or stories, or any other part of these earthly existences without smacking straight into this creature called suffering. He's an unwanted critter, to be sure, who plops into every life worth living, taking on as many different forms as, well, a pod from outer space.

I know this is true, though I wish it weren't.

Even when I was young, I felt tension that suffering brings. In fact, by the time I was about nine years old, I'd already scraped my elbows more times than I could count. I'd gone to the hospital in an ambulance, and I'd felt disappointment's sting on a regular basis. I didn't like any of it. But I had a way to go in understanding a strange and awkward beast like suffering. A long way.

Lynn lived next door to me, one of the few girls on our street and a few years younger than I was. She wasn't much interested in tossing footballs or building forts with me. Still, I was happy enough to have her around and could usually convince her to join me in some level of snowman building or summer bike riding. I remember she laughed a lot, and as she did, her red curly hair bounced around her head like happy springs.

But one winter Saturday I knocked on her door, and her mom told me Lynn wouldn't be able to play for a while. Her daughter had had surgery on her spine to correct its form.

"How come?" I asked.

Because it had grown into the shape of an *S*, she said, and it needed to look like an *I*. Her mom said it would be hard for everyone for a while, but the surgery and the pain now would make Lynn's life better when she got older. She'd be able to stand up as straight as I could.

For the next several months, Lynn was trapped in a white cast from her neck to her hips. She lay in bed unable to move or turn or scoot any direction at all. It was as if she was frozen in pain for half a year, alive but not really, alert but not much. Her eyes were usually shut when I saw her. Her curls lay still on her head because there was not much for a seven-year-old child in a full body cast to laugh about.

I felt bad for my neighbor, but I went on throwing snowballs or circling the neighborhood when the lilacs came. She emerged from those months fragile and weak, but she said she felt happy to be moving at all. Yes, it still hurt. It would take a while to get right.

Her family moved away the next year, and I rode my bike by myself after that. I scraped another knee and then watched another winter roll in. But I soon lost touch with Lynn, and so I never did find out if the suffering she experienced that year really did make her life better.

Anybody who has survived his childhood has enough information about life to last him the rest of his days.
—Flannery O'Connor, *Mystery and Manners: Occasional Prose*

We come out screaming, don't we? We descend onto the world with sobs and wails and piercing awareness that it's not at all like it was only a short time ago. When we were snug, where we were fed and protected. When we didn't have to worry about a single thing except eating and sleeping.

But this place of shadowy halls and drafty rooms and runny noses is different, cold, not cozy. In fact, it feels broken. And the slightest bump only reinforces that brokenness. We don't have to breathe for long to feel the pain.

Still, suffering is confusing. What does it have to do with passionate caring?

After all, we live in a culture devoted to progress and comfortableness. Convenience stores, online shopping, and delivery services make our lives easier. Marketing gurus do everything they can to ensure we're happy—or at least numb—consumers. I don't know of a single travel agent who'd recommend a trip to the Heartbreak Hotel, or any parent who'd send a child to Camp Miserable. It's as if we fight our whole lives to prove the coaches were wrong when they shouted at us: *no pain, no gain.*

We want bike rides or snowmen, not body casts.

For all the hype, though, the reality of a broken world still sits in our living room where it doesn't belong. Each morning, headlines deliver word of war or freak accidents, incurable diseases or school shootings, to remind us that this business of living is anything but easy. It's hard. And if it's not hard on one corner of the planet, you can be sure it will be on another. Teenagers go missing, CEOs hang themselves, or sisters get breast cancer. Babies starve to death, rivers get contaminated, leaders commit adultery. This is a rough place, to be sure, a world that's ugly, mean, discouraging; and most of us can't go more than a few steps in a day without encountering it.

I confess, when the tragedies become too much to read, or the aches in my body too uncomfortable, I flip the pages to the Entertainment section or I grab an Advil. I change the channel or find a new website that's upbeat. I call a friend who's optimistic, because somewhere else, I figure, it's going to be brighter. I want options—strategies even—for avoidance. I step around the creature. And sometimes, when I'm really sad or discouraged or ashamed—and I'm hoping you're in this with me—I'll pop in a DVD, eat a bowl of chocolate ice cream, or drink a beer—anything but feel the tiniest displeasure or sorrow.

Is it a woe of our Western culture, this aversion to discomfort? A universal attribute of our species? Or is my heart more deceitful and delusional than I want to admit?

Maybe the answer is, *all of the above.*

What the answer is not, though, is that suffering is God's idea of a joke, like some kick in the side without a point or a purpose. It's not. God is good. And though I hardly want to believe it, I've suspected for years that being alive is not synonymous with feeling good.

Most things break, including hearts. The lessons of a life amount not to wisdom but to scar tissue and callus.

—Wallace Stegner, The Spectator Bird

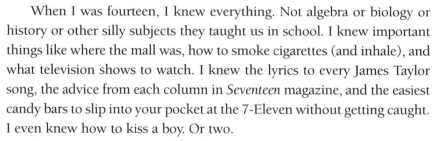

When I was fourteen, I knew everything. Not algebra or biology or history or other silly subjects they taught us in school. I knew important things like where the mall was, how to smoke cigarettes (and inhale), and what television shows to watch. I knew the lyrics to every James Taylor song, the advice from each column in *Seventeen* magazine, and the easiest candy bars to slip into your pocket at the 7-Eleven without getting caught. I even knew how to kiss a boy. Or two.

These were the essential facts for teenage girls in 1973. Survival skills for the suburbs, excitement in a cul-de-sac existence.

Midway through my ninth-grade year, I was having a hard time getting through to the people in my world. My mom and I were only good at yelling at each other; my brothers were absorbed in their girlfriends-of-the-week; and my dad was hard at work at the Pepsi-Cola Bottling Company earning a salary that could pay for our mall visits and ski lessons, television sets and groceries.

I had a few friends who saw things my way, but the adults in my neighborhood were hopeless. They were also good at yelling or pointing or worse, threatening to call my mother whenever I kicked over their plants or teased their children. I'd just shrug my shoulders and move on to the next house.

And my teachers at Manning Junior High were the worst. In fact, I was quite sure they had no natural abilities whatsoever for learning the things I could teach them, so I decided I just wouldn't bother. With any of them.

Miss Nelson, my physical education teacher, found me one morning outside the football shed near the track, smoking a Marlboro Light, when I was supposed to be wearing my blue polyester gym suit jumper and attending her class. Her white hair was cropped close to her ears, and her chin, arms, and belly jiggled when she walked up to me.

"Inside, young lady. Immediately," she said, a bass throttle of a voice. I was nearly finished with my cigarette anyway, so I stamped it against the shed, flicked it on the track, and followed her into the girls' locker room. She stood beside my locker and gave me two choices: either I could change my clothes, put on my uniform, and join the class on the basketball court; or I could go see Mr. Haywood, the principal, and explain what I'd been doing.

I wasn't dumb. She'd just listed way more than two choices, so I simply answered, "No." She interpreted that as defiance, scribbled out a note, and sent me to the principal's office, where I sat by the receptionist in the office until the bell rang. Mr. Haywood was busy in a meeting.

I wandered down the hall to Mr. McPherson's science class. He wasn't as patient as Miss Nelson, so when I rolled up tissues and tossed them at the boys who were poking things in their petri dishes, he simply pointed to the door. I was not welcome in his classroom if I was not interested in science, he hollered, and so I was to leave immediately. He didn't care where I went, just that I did. I picked up my notebook and shrugged again.

An hour later I was sitting in Miss Peters's math class, mimicking her nasal drone to the girls sitting beside me. Each time she tried to explain a problem, I'd copy her voice and caricature her mannerisms. My friends and I would bellow with laughter until finally poor Miss Peters burst into tears and ran out the door. We were still joking and howling when Mr. Haywood suddenly appeared. He marched right over to me, squinted into my face, and whispered, "You. Now."

I sat in a metal chair across from his desk while he picked up the phone. My mom didn't answer his call so he flipped through a file, found my dad's work phone number, and dialed. He explained the situation, discussed my "blatant disrespect for authority," and asked my father to come right away to pick me up. I rolled my eyes and sighed, then I heard him say I was being suspended from school. For three days.

I shook my head. It wasn't fair. I wasn't being treated right. No one had bothered to listen to me, to hear my side. It wasn't my fault school was so boring. But Mr. Haywood simply pointed his index finger toward my eyeballs and dared me to say another word. I flopped my arms across my chest and kicked out my feet. I huffed. And I waited.

About forty-five minutes later, my dad walked in. He looked at me for an eternal second and sat down quietly beside me. Mr. Haywood shut the door. Then the principal gave my dad a few more details about what I had—and had not—done that day. How I had disobeyed my teachers and even upset one so much he wasn't sure she'd come back to work. Clearly

I had problems, he told my father, and he sincerely hoped that three days of punishment would help me sort them out.

My dad took off his glasses and rubbed his eyes. He nodded at Mr. Haywood, and I wondered when he was going to come to my defense, when he was going to rise up and protect me from the injustice that was clearly being inflicted on me. But he didn't say a word. And as I looked at him incredulously, I noticed something that was far worse than any deed I'd committed.

He was crying. Not sobbing or wailing or anything dramatic like that. Just a few tiny tears had slipped down his cheek before he could rub them off, so that we wouldn't see what was happening. My head dropped.

Then my dad cleared his throat. He thanked the principal for his patience, apologized for my behavior, and promised that I would indeed work on my behavior. He turned toward the door and I followed.

We lived only a few miles from my junior high, but it might as well have been a hundred. I had experienced hospital stays during bouts of the measles and flu and lived through my share of athletic injuries and sibling fights. I'd watched seven-year-old Lynn suffer under the heaviness of back surgery. But this was the first time the language of suffering meant more than physical pain. I realized it could hurt more than a twisted ankle or a stomachache, and though no words had registered in my brain those times I'd scraped my elbow, they now landed in my psyche with clarity and meaning.

Beyond a throb or an ache, suffering now had a moral lesson to teach me, a sentence or two scribbled across my conscience. Especially when I heard my dad's quiet voice say in the car, "I'm disappointed, honey, . . . but I know you'll do better."

I spent the next three days moping and wallowing in my lonely suspension at home. I ate potato chips. I watched reruns of *Gilligan's Island*.

I flipped through back issues of *Seventeen*—but nothing helped me feel better. True, I didn't really care that I wasn't in school, but this was an isolation not of my choosing, a sting I could not control.

And no snack food or TV show, no ice pack or aspirin could fix it.

Why must it be pain? Why can't He wake us more gently, with violins or laughter? Because the dream from which we must be awakened is the dream that all is well.

          —William Nicholson, *Shadowlands*

Buddhists call suffering a karmic path of existence. Medieval dramas equate it with a knight's endless agony, tempered only when he's reunited with his beloved maiden. Doctors describe it as an emotional state triggered by biological threats to the individual's integrity. Psychoanalysts suggest it is the result of a feeling of alienation and insurmountable ambivalence, whose aim is to reduce anxiety. Suffering, they conclude, usually accompanies severe pain but may also occur in its absence.

Please, I'd rather not.

But then I hear a different perspective. Like a few weeks ago when I listened to a preacher recount the terrible sufferings to come that are spelled out in the book of Revelation—you know the kind: plagues and curses, diseases and wars. It was hardly an uplifting sermon, but the reverend promised he was not reviewing the litany of agony to depress us. He said, like all of scripture—from floods to fires—this passage was meant as a wake-up call. Take note, he said, of the life we have, the gifts we're given. Pay attention. The apostle Paul counted it pure joy, as if he knew we can't have one without the other—gifts without suffering. Not really.

I want to agree. Granted, it hasn't always been an easy lesson for a middle-class white girl who grew up in a neighborhood where disorder was quickly landscaped and struggle swept into closets of denial. Remember, I lived in a world where I was given novocaine *and* lollipops every time I went to the dentist's office. If my socks wore out, I'd go to the mall for a new pair. And if my soul ached from loneliness, I could always find a way to get noticed by at least a few teachers, even if it wasn't for the best of reasons.

I knew more about being comfortable than I ever did its opposite. Still do. And certainly I'm glad. Grateful even.

But it's complicated, isn't it, this portion of passion? Like a central nervous system in a body, pain shoots through a life—or a lifestyle—and reminds us that there are other forces at work. We're not really in control the way we thought—no matter where we live or who our daddy works for or how resourceful our mom is. No matter how much we medicate ourselves or build cushy padding all around us, suffering has the ability to trample into our lives and wreak all sorts of havoc on what we've come to call *security*.

Whether during the days of suspension at home, in the hospital waiting room, or when I moved into an inner-city neighborhood, I have slowly learned—and relearned—how suffering isn't confined to neighbors with crooked spines, disobedient teenagers, or healthy husbands. It doesn't discriminate, and there is no hierarchy for it, because when you are in the middle of an affliction—regardless of its cause or its effect—all you know is that it hurts.

To draw an analogy: a man's suffering is similar to the behavior of gas. If a certain quantity of gas is pumped into an empty chamber, it will fill the chamber completely and evenly, no matter how big the chamber. Thus suffering completely fills the human soul and conscious mind, no matter whether the suffering is great or little. Therefore, the "size" of human suffering is absolutely relative.

—Viktor Frankl, *Man's Search for Meaning*

I shuffled through the rest of junior high and high school with a little more regard for others and a slightly improved grade point average. (Correction does have its benefits.) It helped that a few other influences were at work as well. When a track coach encouraged me to run and an English teacher inspired me to read, I began to see a purpose behind pain. It wasn't just punishment for bad behavior.

In fact, if my muscles and joints ached, that was a good sign, Coach Haase said. It meant I was getting stronger and more prepared for the next race. If a passage from Frederick Douglass's narrative on slavery upset me, Mrs. Manning said I was "building muscles in my mind." I was becoming better equipped, she told me, to tackle other, more complex stories.

And when Maureen, my youth group leader, said that she'd heard rumors of how belligerent I had been in junior high, she knew she had to pray all the harder for me. God, she'd tell me over breakfast meetings at the Village Inn Pancake House, could bring good from any situation, no matter how difficult it seemed. That was what Christ's life on earth was all about; that was why he had suffered so much himself.

I held on to their words, but it was a flimsy grip. While I was in college, friends slipped into abusive relationships, and my own parents cut off theirs. I entered teaching in the halls of a public high school and heard my students' accounts of drug-addicted mothers and violent fathers. When the teams I began coaching got pummeled, players got injured, or the athletic administrator threatened my contract, I revisited that axiom that *suffering develops character*, which, *ultimately, produces joy*. But when one close friend ended her life, and another ended our fellowship because she was "tired of God," the words about character slipped a notch. Or ten.

Pain was a problem indeed. This grown-up world I now lived in was not nearly so comfortable as the one I'd grown up in. It needed fixing. And nothing instant or convenient would do the trick. So I read some more. Books on city life, science-fiction novels, teaching guides on discipline, organization, or prayer. I watched artsy movies, played women's-league soccer, and visited my parents. I joined a church or two, signed up for Bible-study groups and retreats, hoping each would impart some meaning to this transcendent dilemma.

But instead of escaping it or even understanding it, somehow I entered in more deeply. Not on purpose really. Some parallel movement had been stirring inside me, unexplainable but authentic, and you know already that I couldn't stay put.

I loaded up boxes, packed my car, and I moved. Out of the public high school suburbs and into the city. To a neighborhood brimming with suffering, where broken glass and Section 8 apartments were as common as trimmed bushes and subdivisions had been in mine. Five Points was the historic African-American community of Denver, one-time jazz capital of the West, and just a few miles north of downtown. Its name came from an intersection where five major streets merged, but the joke around town was that anyone who grew up here never went anywhere. It didn't seem very funny.

I moved into an old house that sat about ten yards from an apartment building. The Martin Luther King Jr. Apartments were part of a housing ministry that offered decent and affordable units for low-income families. I'd met most of the children who lived there from an after-school program where I volunteered, and I felt comfortable living next door to them. What was uncomfortable was watching some of their cousins scurry barefoot around the same apartments they shared—five or six kids to a room. Televisions blared in each apartment, while mothers stayed home most days watching them because they couldn't find jobs. Fathers were long gone, the families told me, because they couldn't receive government assistance if there was a man in the house.

Local grocery stores hiked up prices because they knew most goods were bought with food stamps anyway, and children thought joining a gang was a better alternative than Little League. There were no local malls here, no ice-skating rinks nearby, no dentists' offices with lollipops. There were, however, convenience stores on every corner, usually next door to historic houses, churches, and liquor stores.

This was suffering that was unfamiliar to me, the kind that happened because of a lack of resources and choices. The books called it poverty.

And with these economic injustices often came racial tensions and desperate behaviors. I watched white police officers harass black teenagers simply for walking down the streets together. I witnessed desperate mothers tease a landlord's patience just long enough before another eviction notice was slapped on the door and I'd wonder where my neighbors had gone. I made friends with a few homeless men who walked the alleys of our streets back and forth to downtown, and I'd worry on snowy January nights whether they'd be able to keep warm.

It was all very confusing. Especially when I'd drive to the suburbs to teach at a Christian college and people would ask me how the ministry was "down there." As if I lived on the other side of the moon. As if my neighbors were alien creatures compared to my colleagues or students.

This suffering, this problem of economic disparity, of pain and misery and distress, seemed unnecessary. Lynn's surgery would make her life better, her mom said; my junior high punishment had been inflicted to correct my behavior. Those reasons for suffering I could understand. But what was the point in this? Public policies had spiraled into disarray; history's racist residue had divided cities; and now each led to hard choices, harder lifestyles, and collective sorrow. No doubt it was complicated. But where, I thought, was the purpose behind *this*? What possible lesson could there be for this kind of agony? How could anyone live passionately when so much suffering was happening around her?

Where were God's people in all of this? Where were those who followed the Great Physician, those eliminators of suffering, those advocates for the sufferers?

The problems—and questions—were only amplified for me when I moved to Mississippi and saw firsthand history's unkind consequences of the evil known as segregation. In West Jackson, shotgun homes and dilapidated apartment buildings sat literally in the shadow of the Capitol Building, while elegant malls and subdivisions lay miles outside city limits. Here, the lines were clearly drawn. And though meaningful efforts were being made to bring the state's people together, it was slow going. Like the pace of that hot summer I lived there.

In New York, pockets of the city resembled what my husband often called the third world, in part because so many of its people were crammed into spaces not built for such numbers. But living here also meant watching the furthest ends of the spectrum intersect daily—the wealthiest congressional district in the country sat only a few blocks from one of the poorest. Agony walked next to opulence (and in some cases the two were the same). The discrepancies were as vast as the masses of diverse people, which meant you couldn't go anywhere in New York City without bumping into someone's distress.

Pain is not easily hidden in city life.

And the more pavement I pounded, the more another truth came to me, one I suppose that I suspected even before Mr. Haywood's judgment. My urban education instructed me over and over again that I was as capable of causing suffering as I was of feeling it. When push came to shove—and city life can push and shove—I could inflict pain at the same time I could nurse it. I could be a monster tossing out profanities from a selfish heart. And I could be a victim of the same from others.

Neither kind of pain was particularly appealing. But thank God, somewhere along the road, pressed against the teeming urban life, I began to realize I *could* control some matters. Some sufferings could be addressed through creative justice, tenacious ingenuity, or plain old elbow grease. Then again, some could not. Maybe knowing the difference was what my dad meant by "doing better."

Man is great in so far as he realizes that he is wretched. A tree does not know its own wretchedness.

—Blaise Pascal, *Pensées*

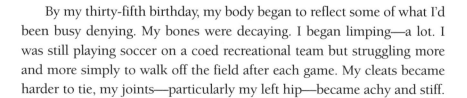

By my thirty-fifth birthday, my body began to reflect some of what I'd been busy denying. My bones were decaying. I began limping—a lot. I was still playing soccer on a coed recreational team but struggling more and more simply to walk off the field after each game. My cleats became harder to tie, my joints—particularly my left hip—became achy and stiff.

Once I finally forced myself to visit the doctor, I heard the bad news: I had advanced arthritis and would qualify immediately for a hip replacement. A what?! Though I was a youthful thirty-five years old, the doctor told me I would probably not make it to my fortieth birthday before I'd be unable to walk normally or enjoy the quality of life I'd been used to.

To hear him pronounce the diagnosis hurt more than my hip at the time. It was a stab at my sense of control, which turned into a bruise on my ego. How could I live well, live fully and passionately, when it was just a matter of time before the pain would become chronic and excruciating? What would I do if the dead weight I'd be forced to carry and manage would keep me from the passions that defined me?

I tried to adjust. The next year I replaced jogging with bike riding. The next, I walked less and read more; and the one after that, I sat in the lodge of the ski resort rather than tackle the moguls of a slope. I ate more green and less white. I asked friends to pray for me and swallowed an array of vitamins to supplement their prayers, in hopes that either—or both—might work, and I'd be healed. Most days I pretended I was fine by stepping around the creature, ignoring my limp and my pain only until someone asked about either. Eventually I gave up even on divine intervention and mustered all I could to bear up under the burden and limits of an arthritic condition. I was never going to be the same.

Which, of course, was bad and good.

Following one Christmas dinner, eleven years after that diagnosis, I went for a walk—a slow stroll really—with my husband's family. Piercing bolts shot through me from my hip to my toes and back again. My limp and my face must have reflected the pain, because my sister-in-law asked the obvious: "Why don't you get that fixed? What are you waiting for?"

Courage, I thought. I was waiting to become brave enough to subject myself for the first time in my life to surgery. I wasn't dumb: I knew they cut you in surgery and you bleed, two experiences I'd become adept at avoiding whenever possible. I was also waiting for some ingenious new technology that might replace my battered joint with merely the wave of a wand, without an incision or a trip to a doctor. Or maybe I was waiting for the prayers to be answered because that would be the easiest and definitely the most spiritual.

Whichever my reasons for delaying the inevitable, after one too many sleepless nights and humiliating moments when my husband had to tie my shoes for me because I couldn't reach the laces, I gave in. I couldn't even bend over to clip my toenails. I was taking ibuprofen with my vitamins each morning because I couldn't walk more than a few blocks without needing to sit down. I became so desperate I began to listen: "God loves us, so He makes us the gift of suffering," said the playwright William Nicholson in *Shadowlands.*

> Through suffering, we release our hold on the toys of this world, and know our true good lies in another world. We're like blocks of stone, out of which the sculptor carves the forms of men. The blows of His chisel, which hurt us so much, are what make us perfect. The suffering in the world is not the failure of God's love for us; it is that love in action. For believe me, this world that seems to us so substantial is no more than the shadowlands. Real life has not begun yet.

Armed with a tempered passion, I prepared. I found an orthopedic surgeon near our home, scheduled the date, and, almost a year from that Christmas stroll, my husband drove me to the hospital. There was nothing pleasant or comfortable about it. There was no joy in lying in a hospital bed, completely dependent on the help of others for warmth and food and you know what. My body ached, my energy drained. Five days later I came home with stitches in my skin, a new steel-and-ceramic joint in my hip, and a new appreciation for the creativity of medical artists.

To think about it now, I can't believe I really went ahead with it. Or that I live in a time when medical research has advanced to the place where joints can be replaced, clogged arteries can be bypassed, and cancer can be treated. Or on a continent where I can now make it to fifty standing up straight and going for long walks with my husband after dinner.

I only know the surgery—and the pain—really did make me better.

Many people seem to think it foolish, even superstitious, to believe that the world could still change for the better. And it is true that in winter it is sometimes so bitingly cold that one is tempted to say, "What do I care if there is a summer; its warmth is no help to me now." Yes, evil often seems to surpass good. But then, in spite of us, and without our permission, there comes at last an end to the bitter frosts. One morning the wind turns, and there is a thaw. And so I must still have hope.

—Vincent van Gogh

I heard the laughter of hope. Not loud or wild or obnoxious. Just soft and sure and full.

It was the joy of children playing on our city street with the old bicycle rim they'd found in the alley. They nailed it to a telephone poll and tossed a deflated basketball through it like they were champions.

It was the abiding grace of neighbors cooking a batch of corn bread and fried chicken with provisions they'd bought with their food stamps.

It was the humility in a pulpit that reminded me of the Word made flesh.

It was the simple knock on the door from an unemployed mother who had the time to visit and encourage.

It was the courage of a friend whose regular migraine headaches rarely kept her from singing and cooking and praying for faraway friends. Like me.

It was the resolve, dreams, and generosity of those who should have been anything but resolved or generous given their circumstances, given the immensity of pain they endured.

It was this other side of suffering, this song in the fields, sung loudest as the temperatures rose, that I've marveled at over the years. It laughs quietly, confidently. Because, somehow, pain feeds the delight for living.

Pain instructs and ignites, sculpts and prods, reminding us of the extravagant gifts of pain-free hips, gracious parents, and passion-filled friends. Somehow, pain creates a ridiculous gratitude that emerges in spite of the wretchedness around us. Or within us.

Of course, that doesn't mean I'll invite the pesky critter along on my next trip. Nor am I any more excited by its presence. I still find suffering confusing and am not any the wiser about its insidious power on human souls. No, the habits of delusion I've spent a lifetime developing, the strategies I've cooked up for avoiding anything that hurts, are not easily purged.

I can't deny—and all the more with each day's newspaper I read—that tragedy, suffering, illness, or pain can pop up at any moment of any day in any shape. Still, as it does, a heart can become frigid or it can begin to thaw. We can reach for another blanket or we can move into the sun. It is a gift. Or it is a burden. Or it is both. Neither is easy, but both deepen our reason for living. For risking and loving. For moving at all and keeping awake.

There's no getting around the creature. Because C. S. Lewis was right: "We were promised sufferings. They were part of the program. We were even told, 'Blessed are they that mourn.'" So we might as well acknowledge the blessed beast for what it is: an elephant with a purpose. And a very big shadow.

The tears of all things are swallowed up
in the glad triumph of God.
—Ralph C. Wood,
"Shadowlands," a review

---

pas·sion (pāshʹən) n. [Middle English, from
Old French, from Medieval Latin passio, pas-
sion-, *sufferings of Jesus or a martyr*, from
Late Latin, *physical suffering, martyrdom, sin-*
ful desire, from Latin, *an undergoing*, from
passus, past participle of *pati*, to suffer; see
pe(i)- in Indo-European roots.]

The sufferings of Jesus in the period
following the Last Supper and including
the Crucifixion, as related in the New
Testament.

Six

Broken Lambs

and the debts I can never pay

Our life is made by the death of others.
—Leonardo da Vinci

These days, I live in a town that's built around its cemeteries. Houses, shops, and restaurants sprinkle the borders of these New England grave-yards, and most of the town's streets converge at their various entrances. As grandmothers relax on their porches or families sit down to dinner, they glance out over crooked tombstones and weathered markers to watch a tired sun drop slowly from the sky. Death at the center of life.

Because these graveyards spread across a half dozen miles of hills with asphalt paths, I walk (quite quickly and easily these days, I might add) or pedal my bicycle around them for daily exercise. Sometimes the winter cold slaps my face, or the windy autumns zap my energy. Most days, though, no matter the season, I don't want to go. And when I do, I can't go more than a few yards before I want to quit, go back up the steps to my living room, and stretch out on my couch. I'd rather exercise my mind (or my jaw) than my body. But I go anyway, and when I do, my lungs ache for air, my muscles burn for reprieve, my emotions battle with ego, until I look up and see the quiet shadows of human stories around me, whispering for me to keep riding. Keep going.

Life infused by death.

How often I have watched—and participated in—the pattern, established two thousand years ago, of human activity swirling around a dying moment, of glancing at the inevitable only from a distance. I'll be honest: I do not want my heart to stop beating, or my blood to stop flowing in my veins, or my joints to stop moving—even if the moving is hard. These days all the more, I wake up to feel age's gravity pull at my bones and muscles, while hindsight shows me the regrets of countless battles, bad decisions, and missed words that have littered my journey. I try to hold them at bay. Or at least in perspective. After all, in my mind, I am still twelve years old holding my kitten, or thirty-eight years old holding a camera on vacation in Ireland. Degeneration—both physical and spiritual—is still something that happens to *other* people. Even if my hip tells me otherwise. Even if I stare at my husband's living, breathing, sunburned face.

I'm a slow believer. So I don't think much about death because I don't understand how to live with it, even if reminders of it surround me.

It's harder still to fully believe how the excruciating end of one life could become the beginning of measureless living for another, how blood spilled once in Jerusalem somehow heals the aches of restless souls.

But it does. It is the true story of Passion, placed in a sacred week for holy and sinful people to enter through the centuries, that calls me now. A historic truth from which all other elements of living derive their meaning: a wandering nomad becomes the focus of all art, the secret to vocation, the heart behind each romance, and the link to every type of suffering.

"I have come that they may have life, and have it to the full," the Passion said.

But because I am not very good at believing, I need memories and markers and a lot of help from others just to get going.

Life is a great surprise. I do not see why death should not be an even greater one.

—Vladimir Nabokov, *Pale Fire*

I began hounding my mother to give me a cat when I was ten years old. For two years, my brothers and I had shared the responsibilities of dropping puppy cereal into the bowls of our two dachshunds, Yatzee and Baron, during which time I developed a healthy dose of caregiving confidence. I had changed enough water bowls, scooped up enough dog poop, and brushed enough brown hair off their little backs to know that I was capable of animal maintenance. So when I turned ten years old, I sat my mom down on the sofa in our living room, looked her square in the face, and informed her of my decision to get a new pet.

She said no.

I spent the next months moping behind the miniature dogs, complaining of their laziness, and pushing them out of the way with my foot each time I opened the refrigerator. They were boring, I told my mom; the wiener dogs were unadventurous, fat, selfish. All they did was eat, bark, sleep, and make messes I had to clean up, because by then my brothers were busy with girlfriends and football practices. I deserved better, I told her. I deserved a cat.

"We'll see," she said one Saturday.

It wasn't much, but it was all the hope I needed.

Our neighbors around the corner owned a gentle gray Siamese who was pregnant. One school night they stopped by to see if we might want to take one of the kittens from the litter. Of course, they weren't sure when the kittens would be born or how many their cat would have, but they said we could have first pick if we wanted one before they put an ad in the *Weekly Sentinel*. I hovered around my mother like a mosquito, picking at her wrist and tapping on her shoulder until finally she peeled my body off hers and told the neighbors to call us when the kittens arrived.

I set up camp around the telephone. Each time it rang, my heart got lodged in my throat, and I'd barely squeak out a *Hello*. Then I'd wait a few seconds in anticipation until I heard the voices of everyone in the world *except* the cat neighbors and pass the phone to my mom in a despair worthy of Anne of Green Gables. Yatzee and Baron had not recovered their appeal, so I cleared a space between the piles of clothes on the floor in my room for the kitten, just in case. I even began reading about litter boxes and dawdled in the pet food aisle every time I accompanied my mom to the grocery store.

The call came one night when I was scooping up after the minidogs. My mom told me to get in the car. We drove a few blocks, parked, and walked up the sidewalk to the yellow brick house of hope.

"You can pick it out, honey," my mom was saying as I skipped ahead. "Just remember, you're responsible for this animal."

I was ready. I looked over the scrawny five and picked the littlest and scrawniest of the bunch, the one the neighbors said probably wasn't going to make it. I knew a challenge when I heard one and was so sure of my invincibility by then that life hereafter was going to be grand for all animals everywhere. Or at least all cats in my house.

I named my tiny silver kitten Jeorge, with a *J* instead of a *G* because everyone in my suburban family had a first name that began with *J*—Jack, Jan, Jim, John, and me. I didn't care that my dad said the cat was proba-bly a girl. It was only right that this new member had a *J*-name as well, and Jeorge was as good as any. I fed her squished-up bread dipped in milk for the first few days and teased her with a piece of yarn, which she'd bat with a paw no bigger than my thumb. We set up a small box of sand in the laundry room, and I'd drop her in anytime she arched her back or whenever she'd leave puddles on the kitchen floor. Whichever came first.

Soon Jeorge was finding her own way to the box, throwing a friendly punch at Yatzee or Baron whenever they weren't sleeping, and even lick-ing the water from her own bowl. Because of the squirrels and alley cats in our neighborhood, we decided life would be better for Jeorge if she remained a house cat, so my mom made arrangements with the vet to have Jeorge's claws removed. That would keep the couches pretty and the kitten gentle for a long time, my mom told me.

She was right too. We never did get a new sofa, even after I left for college years later. And I marveled at Jeorge's gentleness every day. I fed her, brushed her, and scooped out her box with regular care, making her new home cozy and safe. I loved Jeorge.

About a year after bringing her home, I woke up one morning to find Jeorge hanging her head over the laundry room sink. She sat on the win-dowsill above it, lifeless and gray, watching the slow drip of the faucet as if she knew she needed a drink but she couldn't quite reach it. I picked her up and placed her head over her water bowl. She did not move. I bounced a piece of yarn in front of her face, but she would hardly acknowledge it, let alone swat at it. Something was wrong.

I held Jeorge in my lap as my mom drove us to the vet for the second time in her life. The veterinarian was convinced that Jeorge's lethargy was a result of some strange disease she had probably acquired from being outside. Only problem was she hadn't been outside—except between the house and the car—so he scratched his head, examined every whisker and hair on her body, and said, "Well, I'm going to have to perform exploratory surgery on her." He went on to tell us that if he couldn't find what was wrong, he'd have to put her to sleep because she probably wouldn't be able to survive the surgery.

He didn't fool me. I knew that "putting her to sleep" didn't have anything to do with sleeping, and I wasn't going for it. I picked up Jeorge, marched right back out to our station wagon, and waited for my mom. Jeorge was not going through some silly surgery, and she certainly was not getting *that* kind of sleep. That is, if I had anything to do with it.

My mom sighed as she climbed into the car. "Honey, are you sure? The vet is a doctor. He probably knows what's best for Jeorge."

No, he doesn't, I told her in one breath. I did. Jeorge would be okay because I would take care of her. Jeorge stared at me with her sky-blue eyes, hoping I would be right.

When we got home, I stayed with Jeorge all night, dropping milk in her mouth with an eyedropper and stroking her soft, lethargic body. I did the same thing the next day and the next. One morning I woke up and Jeorge was licking water out of her bowl by herself! She was chasing Yatzee down the hall, sharpening her clawless paws on the couch, and brushing sand over a mess she'd just made. I was ecstatic. My mom said it was a miracle.

"Funny how a little tender loving care can make a difference," she told me.

And for the next few years, Jeorge became a regular member of our family right down to reflecting Kadlecek traits: stubbornness, independence, playfulness. She slept on my bed or on the Ping-Pong table, chased the dogs around the basement, and regularly explored the kitchen counters whenever my mom was thawing hamburger. Jeorge grew on us.

But like most preteens, I soon took my life with Jeorge for granted. My attention turned to softball games and friends. Scooping Jeorge's sandbox became lower and lower on my priority list, and often my mom had to dish out the canned tunalike cat food for my grown-up kitten because I would forget.

Human care is never enough. It begs for mercy.

One day as I ran out to gossip with a boy down the street, I did not close the screen door all the way. It inched back and forth with the Colorado breeze and created a space big enough for a small animal to crawl through. Especially a curious one who had been neglected by her friend.

I was on the corner when I watched a big green Plymouth drive by. And I was chatting away, tossing blades of grass into the wind when I heard the tires squeal to a stop. I ran toward the noise to see what had happened and saw a woman kneeling in front of her car. I looked up, saw that the car was stopped in front of our house, and watched my mother running—slow motion–like—down our stairs, her hand over her mouth. When I got closer to her, I saw her eyes filled with water and I heard the soft moan of compassion flow out of her mouth in a single word: "Jeorge."

We arrived at the Plymouth at the same time. The driver-woman was mumbling the words "I'm so sorry" over and over like it was an Eastern chant. I clinched my jaw as I looked at the motionless cat on the street and stooped down to the pavement beside her. I said nothing. I cradled my pet in my arms and rose slowly to my feet. Jeorge's neck bobbed back and forth with each step I took. Her head hung over my wrist, and I noticed a tiny spot of blood on her mouth. She was no longer scrawny or little like she was when I first brought her home. She was fat and silver and soft.

And now she really was asleep. Because of me.

Before then, death had not come near my typical suburban existence. All I knew of life was spaghetti with hamburger, Christmas trees with presents, and playful pets with family status. I did not understand dying, especially when I was responsible for it.

I should have done more. I could have.

What I did understand was that Jeorge was not going to wake up. Ever. She was never going to nap on my bed or lick milk off my finger or chase the dogs around the couch. I would never feel her soft coat again or hear her grumbling purr. My scrawny, unlikely, stubborn friend was gone.

My mom gave me a clear plastic shoebox from her closet. I placed Jeorge inside, dug a three-foot hole underneath my window in the yard, and buried my first pet. I scooped dirt one last time for Jeorge and covered her makeshift coffin. Then I tied two sticks together to form a cross, apologized to Jeorge, and said good-bye as I stuck the cross into the ground.

I have often wondered how the next owners of the house must have reacted when they uncovered a feline skeleton in a plastic shoebox underneath a bedroom window. But I have never questioned how Jeorge got there in the first place.

I left the door open.

How we spend our days is, of course, how we spend our lives.
—Annie Dillard, The Writing Life

I have never been to Jerusalem. Never traveled to the Holy Land, though many friends who have been claim their lives will never be the same. They tell me it is an astonishing experience to be on the same soil where Jesus lived and died and lived again. Extraordinary, like nothing else in all the world, they claim. I don't doubt they're right.

Though I've never felt the Sea of Galilee roll over my feet or stood on the same shore where Christ's toes touched the sand, and though I've never traveled the streets of Nazareth or climbed the Mount of Olives where Jesus asked God to reconsider their plan, I suspect these too would be humbling adventures.

I *have* been on the road to Emmaus, that is, Emmaus, Pennsylvania, just north of Philadelphia, where lush trees and small towns line the highway. But I don't think it's quite the same as the road where the Gospel writers say a resurrected Christ chatted with his friends.

And Calvary, or *Golgotha* in Aramaic, "the Place of the Skull," where nails shattered human veins and excruciating executions lingered for days; no, I've never seen that Skull, the one that scholars say was visible from the city, near its gate and next to an easily accessible road.

Reality, however, is not confined to a map, just as a story lives well beyond its words on a page or in a memory.

And so, thankfully, the account of Jesus Christ's death is not reduced to tours or vacations, paper or books. Though I have not heard with my own ears the early cries of the crowds to "crucify him, crucify him," I have chanted it enough throughout my life to know the history of Grace has not died with the times, nor is it owned by any place.

The most famous of all deaths is a Story that lives.

Of course, all stories are water to humans. They are fuel for tired bones, guidance for wandering minds, friendship for lonely humans regardless of age. They bring us delight, move us to reflect, and sharpen our sense of living. They linger at the door each morning we leave for work, offering a breakfast of meaning as to why we're going in the first place.

But the Passion Story, the dying of God in ripped flesh, the center from which all other passions evolve, this is a different story altogether. It is present behind gifted creativity. It is power beside frail hope. It is purpose beyond earthly efforts. As Tolkien suggests: "There is no tale ever told that men would rather find was true, and none which so many sceptical men have accepted as true on its own merits. . . . This story is supreme; and it is true. Art has been verified."

And each time it is told—whether across a stage at Easter, at a dinner table at sunset, or in a statue in a museum—once-sleeping souls begin to stir.

> *I carried my sketchbook and drawing pencils wherever I went, but I remember that the first time I saw the Michelangelo* Pietà *in the Duomo I could not draw it. . . . I stared at its Romanesque and Gothic contours, at the twisted arm and bent head, at the circle formed by Jesus and the two Marys, at the vertical of Nicodemus—I stared at the geometry of the stone and felt the stone luminous with strange suffering and sorrow. I was an observant Jew, yet that block of stone moved through me like a cry, like the call of seagulls over morning surf, like—like the echoing blasts of the shofar sounded by the Rebbe. . . . I do not remember how long I was there that first time. When I came back out into the brightness of the crowded square, I was astonished to discover that my eyes were wet.*
>
> —Chaim Potok, *My Name Is Asher Lev*

Five years after my guilt-laden and, thus far, only encounter with death, I heard for the first time this story of Christ's death. If it had been told to me the few times our family attended Shepherd of the Hills

Presbyterian Church, I had not listened enough for it to register any meaning with me. Church to me was a dull exercise in avoiding arguments with my parents; it was not a balm for a suburban teenage girl who confused loneliness with independence. Besides, I didn't even know what a shepherd was.

By the time I entered high school and my days melted into adolescent insecurity, the hole in my heart began nagging me. I felt everything *but* invincible by then, though I was hardly able to articulate that. Self-awareness is not a common attribute for suburban youth, and so I floated between diaries and friends, guitar lessons and English classes like a specter in a Dickens tale hoping some tiny spark—of anything—would ignite my days but never really believing it would.

I might as well have hung my head over the laundry sink. Lethargy for me was becoming a way of life.

When my oldest brother told me about a weekend camp for high school students in the mountains, and my parents were busy with tennis and work the same weekend, I thought it couldn't hurt to sign up. I figured it would give me something to do that probably wasn't boring. I might even find something to care about.

"Have fun, honey," my mom hollered as she dropped me off at the bus. I watched her drive away, even after I could not see her car.

Four hours later we pulled into a gravel parking lot at the foot of a mountain, and I joined a hundred other insecure teens who strolled off the buses pretending we were not self-conscious. We were assigned to little groups and told we would share western-style cabins with the same group of girls or boys. Each group included a few college students acting as counselors. We were told the schedule and when we should be where. And why it all mattered: they wanted us to "have a great time." That was the goal.

What they didn't tell me was that we had to sing quirky songs and listen to some old guy (in his forties) talk for about an hour Saturday morning and then again on Saturday night. I snoozed through most of the morning session and sweated through the pressure of group relays in the snow that afternoon, tripping over teammates and making a mess of the competition. By dinner my limbs were numb, my mouth dry, though I couldn't quite reach the glass of water on the table. But water was hardly the thing I was thirsty for.

Maybe this wasn't such a good idea. Maybe it was.

After dinner, the guy told us to get comfortable because he was going to tell us a story, one that could very well affect the rest of our lives. A story all of history was wrapped around, one that countless people in countless places had responded to as if they had just heard the best news they could ever have imagined.

And he began: a carpenter named Jesus lived a long time ago. His mission was love, and he wandered the countryside helping people and wanting nothing more than to care for their souls. I perked up.

Often this carpenter would say things that upset the local leaders, though he always spoke truth with perfect love. One day he went too far, though, and was betrayed by a friend, thrown into the hands of corrupt leaders who stripped off his clothes and tore open his back with sharp pieces of lead tied to leather strands. They crammed thorns shaped like a crown into his head, so hard that blood spilled onto his face and dried. Then they tossed him back and forth between punches like he was a criminal. Except he wasn't. And he never opened his mouth to defend himself.

I was caught.

The leaders and guards then ordered the exhausted, bleeding man to pick up a huge wooden cross twice his size and drag it down the city streets where crowds of people had by now lined up like they were watching a parade. Somehow he made it to the hill not far from town and would have collapsed except he was first pushed on top of the cross. Soldiers hammered long, square nails into his wrists and feet, fastening him to the cross. Then they heaved this cross into the ground, hoisting the carpenter ten or so feet off the ground, so that his lungs eventually would collapse and his heart would burst. This man who helped people, who cared for them with all his being, now was experiencing one of the most barbaric forms of execution.

And suddenly, my fifteen-year-old eyes watched him in that dark place and felt the chill of terror go up my spine. I saw the blood on his cheeks, smelled the death all around him, and trembled when the life went out of a man I had met only forty minutes ago.

"And he did this for you." The guy looked square into my face, and I heard the soft moan of compassion flow out of his mouth: "So *you* would never have to be lonely again."

How did he know?

"That's how much he loves you."

I stared hard at the Story in front of me. Love *me*? I was not exactly the picture of lovableness. I barely earned a B-average in school, played every position in softball because I wasn't good at any one, and was not naturally inclined to caring for anyone but myself. I had discovered that especially five years earlier and had been relearning it ever since. Now the speaker-guy was inviting me to a life of love I would never have imagined but always hoped for.

What did I have to do? I wondered.

"And the only thing you have to do," he said out loud, "is believe."

But I should do more. I could.

The guy was bowing his head along with everyone else in the room. I know: I watched. Then I walked outside, stared at the Colorado stars, and thought a long time about the death of Jesus. It was a story I could not resist. A true story where death helped a young life matter.

> *[The disciples] had seen the strong hands of God twist the crown of thorns into a crown of glory, and in hands as strong as that they knew themselves safe. They had misunderstood practically everything Christ had ever said to them, but no matter: the thing made sense at last, and the meaning was far beyond anything they had dreamed. They had expected a walkover, and they beheld a victory; they had expected an earthly Messiah, and they beheld the Soul of Eternity.*
>
> —Dorothy L. Sayers, "The Triumph of Easter," in *Letters to a Diminished Church*

No matter how many books you read on the subject, how many paintings you've studied, or how many war movies you might have watched, there is nothing as profoundly incomprehensible as watching another living being take his or her final breath on this planet. To see the slow strength of life evaporate from a body just inches from yours is the most astonishing paradox you will ever know: the pain pierces every part of you and yet, the privilege of being close enough to feel the warm flesh is equally piercing.

It is the most horrible of gifts.

And it is utter despair without another Death to help you make sense of it.

Each morning when I wake up here in our New England home, I glance at a small photograph of a lamb that sits neatly atop my dresser. The lamb's wool is dirty white, its ears pressed back behind its head, and its face the size of a child's outstretched hand. Its legs seem no longer than a shoebox, and its mouth clutches a thin white bottle of milk as the lamb sucks its nourishment for the day's survival.

My mother is also in the picture, cradling the lamb against her chest; her left hand holds the glass bottle. You can see her full smile if you look closely at the picture, though it is almost hidden behind the lamb's ear. Still, there is no mistaking that the sixty-something-year-old woman knows how to care for this innocent animal.

I took the photo of my mother and the lamb over a decade ago. She and I were traveling together on vacation to Australia, New Zealand, and Fiji, and this particular day had been a rainy one just outside Christchurch, New Zealand. My mom took this trip Down Under on a regular basis, working as a tour guide for specialized vacations, and she wanted to show me one of her favorite places on earth: a sheep ranch.

She loved the fact that we had to travel by boat across a bay to reach this lonely place where only a few families had cared for sheep for three generations. They'd raise the tame creatures exclusively to shear them, to sell their wool to Americans who came to visit, like us. My mother knew the ranchers by name, and they greeted her as though she was a long-lost aunt finally coming home. They beamed when they showed her their newest arrival, and my mother responded to the small, soft animal in a way she often had responded to me throughout my life: she picked it up gently and fed it. Delighted.

And I grabbed my camera, to hold the memory, I suppose, though I could not have known at the time why I needed to. For years I had tried to tell my mother the story of another Lamb, the one I first heard twenty years earlier. With well-meaning vigor, albeit insensitive tactics, I walked my mom down the same road I had watched the suffering Christ stumble on, trying with all the religious gusto I could find to convince her of the greatest story I had ever heard. I wanted nothing more than to make it as irresistible for her as it had been for me many times since.

It was good news, after all.

In other words, I was hoping to hand my mother a glass of water; instead, ever since my mountain camp weekend, she insisted that she wasn't thirsty. Period. Then she'd respond with shrugged shoulders and a pat on my back.

"That's nice for you, honey, but it's not really for me," she'd say. And she'd begin to talk about sales at the mall or her next trip Down Under.

Now I had spent three weeks—that is, twenty-one days around the clock—touring with her the sites of this land on the other side of the world, this culture she fit into like it was a second home. At her expense. Just so she could show her only daughter the places and people that mattered most to her. She wanted, finally, to show me what a shepherd was.

But foolishness is not easily outgrown for suburban youth who turn into adults. And so today I stare at the photograph, knowing I could have, should have, done more.

Less than a year before I wrote this, I received the phone call that my mom had been taken to the hospital. It was a crisp September day on the East Coast where my husband and I were living, but the news made the air heavy and thick. I called the hospital and was connected to my mom's room. She told me she'd fallen in the night after weeks of feeling like she had the flu, couldn't get back into bed, and had a neighbor help her the next morning.

She lay motionless on the floor in her bedroom—the image still haunts me—and now on the hospital phone she was wondering if I could come out to Denver to be with her. To care for her.

I flew out the next day and stayed with her at the hospital. By the end of September she was in another hospital, getting more tests, and by

October the doctors had determined it was cancer, lymphoma they thought, the kind that attacks a body quickly. She lay still in the bed, her throat dry all the time, her breathing short and hard.

My mom was not getting better. The woman who took me all over the world was struggling now just to go to the toilet.

My oldest brother flew in shortly after I had returned to New York. One morning she told him she had had a dream, one where she knew she was dying but she wasn't buying the reality of it. She asked him what he thought it meant and when she did, my brother pulled a chair in close to her bed, leaned over, and did what he had to do: he told her a story.

Jesus suffered too, so she wouldn't have to, he told her gently as he sat under the fluorescent hospital lights. Christ's love for her was so deep and so enormous that he willingly embraced death so that she could know life everlasting. And three days after his execution on the cross, he became alive again. Death could not keep him in the grave. It was that simple, he explained.

And this time she listened.

She called the next morning to offer me the words I never expected to hear in my unbelieving life: "Honey, I asked God to forgive my sins and now I'm a Christian." I said nothing. Then, before I could think about it, I erupted into a laughter so rich and so full that I began to feel a little like you do when you've just sipped the last drop of wine from a really good bottle. She did too.

The Lamb that was slain became the cornerstone of a whole new story.

What people don't realize is how much religion costs. They think faith is a big electric blanket, when of course it is the cross. It is much harder to believe than not to believe. If you feel you can't believe, you must at least do this: keep an open mind. Keep it open toward faith, keep wanting it, keep asking for it, and leave the rest to God.

— Flannery O'Connor, *The Habit of Being*

My husband and I boarded the plane a week later, hoping to help my mom transition to a nursing home for treatment. Instead, we arrived to learn that she'd been moved to a hospice. A home that made dying comfortable.

No riding around it.

For the next week we gathered around her bed, remembering family vacations and Easter baskets, singing songs and taping roses to her wall. I can still smell the lilac lotion she put on her face, a scent I grabbed every time I kissed her cheek and whispered in her ear how glad I was that she was my mom. I wanted her to die knowing she'd been loved. I wanted to take back all the selfish times I hadn't cared for her like I should have. Like I could have.

I sat as close as I could to her, listening to the rhythm of her breathing, helping her sip some water from a straw, holding her hand and begging for mercy. My husband sat beside me; so did my brothers and sister-in-law, aunt and uncle, even my father, all of us surrounding my mom like a shield. And we waited. And listened some more. And begged a lot for mercy. Abundantly.

Then the nurse checked my mom's pulse, looked at us, and in a gentle moan of compassion, said, "It's okay now. She's gone."

I stared at my mom's empty body, still not understanding what death meant to those who continued to live in this place. I'm not sure I ever will. I did know, though, that I would never be able to hear her voice on the phone or smell the lilacs with her again. And I'd never be able to snap another photograph of her. My mother was not going to wake up again. At least not here.

I ran from the room out into the November air and cried and howled with every part of my being. I walked all around the hospice in the Denver night, my limbs numb, my soul thirsty. I prayed for hope, felt the winter cold stroke my face, and stared long and hard at the stars above me. Then I returned to my family.

And do you know what we did? We told stories. Of the time my mom said this, of the time she did that. Of a dozen uniting minutes we'd shared during the last two weeks of her life. Of the grace of the caregivers in that place and of the generosity of mercy we encountered from friends and strangers. My oldest brother looked me square in the face, smiled, and said, "She's home now."

I knew what he meant. And I know it still each morning I wake up and see my mom holding her lamb.

The joy can never be spoken, above all joys beside,
When in Thy body broken I thus with safety hide.
O Lord of Life, desiring Thy glory now to see,
Beside Thy cross expiring, I'd breathe my soul to Thee.

My Savior, be Thou near me when death is at my door;
Then let Thy presence cheer me, forsake me nevermore!
When soul and body languish, oh, leave me not alone,
But take away mine anguish by virtue of Thine own.

—"O Sacred Head, Now Wounded," a Passion hymn

There are those who say that the cross of Jesus Christ is just a symbol. That his death is simply a boundary marker between BC and AD or an emblem erected over the graves of kings and heroes. Some people in history used the cross merely as a staff to guard their flocks or families, while others fell down prostrate at it, believing it was a god of rain or winds.

There is the legend about the emperor Constantine on his way to Rome: he claimed he saw a luminous cross in the sky with the motto "By this sign conquer." The night before his battle of Saxaruba in 312, the emperor had a dream in which he was to inscribe the cross and the motto on the shields of his soldiers. He did, and his men won the battle.

Even history's unlikely voices recognized the power of the cross. Having fought countless battles and faced untold hardships, the French general Napoleon Bonaparte couldn't help but be confounded by the legacy of the Passion: "Alexander, Caesar, Charlemagne, and myself founded empires; but [upon] what foundation did we rest the creations of our genius? Upon force. Jesus Christ founded an empire upon love; and at this hour millions of men would die for Him."

From where I sit today as a citizen of that empire, I can see that the cross is both a sacred symbol and a protective shield in a world where humans long for both. But it is more than that, just as Jesus himself is more than a war-less leader of old. He is the Last Supper, Good Friday, *and* Easter morning, after all, all of which remind us of a truth and a time when God's passion marked human history, when almighty suffering displayed the deepest love a life could know, when hope's flesh split across hell for every sin-sick soul.

Like me.

There are no more "could haves" for us to carry. We can never *earn* a story, because a story is always offered and then heard, given, and received; its bones, its plot, its protagonist, its power—all a gift. And a sacred nudge to keep breathing fully.

So it is freedom to hang on to each word, to visit the tomb where death first lost its sting, to listen to the Story that is so alive we can't help but remember it, even as we walk by crooked tombstones in the winter cold.

Pain, then, is part of this happiness, now.
That's the deal.
—Joy Gresham to C. S. Lewis in
Shadowlands

---

com·pas·sion (kəm-pāsh´ən) Middle English
compassioun, from Late Latin compassio,
compassion-, from compassus, past participle of compati, to sympathize : Latin com-,
com- + Latin **pati, to suffer**; see pe(i)- in
Indo-European roots] noun.

A powerful, deep awareness of someone
else's suffering, in such a way that you want
that person not to suffer; root is the same as
that of *passion*, something you want so
much that you suffer from not doing or
having or accomplishing it.

The root meaning "to suffer" used of Christ
en route to his crucifixion.

The humane quality of understanding the
suffering of others and wanting to do something about it.

SEVEN

Compassion's Call

and the hands I want to hold

You have been my friend. . . . That in itself is a tremendous thing. . . .
By helping you, perhaps I was trying to lift up my life a trifle.
Heaven knows anyone's life can stand a little of that.
—Charlotte to Wilbur, in *Charlotte's Web* by E. B. White

It was a small thing. She probably wouldn't remember it if you asked her today. But for me, as a young girl who sometimes felt lonely more than I felt loved, this one simple act dropped an entirely new world into my soul.

Our family was visiting my mother's father and sisters in California one summer vacation. They took us for a drive to a vineyard, and as soon as we parked, my brothers, my parents, and the others were off exploring. I'd barely gotten out of the car when I realized I was behind them all. One of my aunts, though, stayed with me. So I stepped beside her and sighed, not sure why my brothers had abandoned me or why we were at this stupid vineyard in the first place.

She didn't give me much time to sulk. At first, we skipped to catch up. Then we slowed down, and suddenly my aunt stopped. I did too. She shushed me and pointed toward something. I looked but couldn't see what she saw. So she turned my shoulders, stood behind me, and bent in real close, one hand on my shoulder and the other gesturing in the direction of the bird to make sure I saw it. And there it was. Little, dark, and fluttering. We smiled. And though it was hot outside that day, I remember I got chills.

But I'll be honest with you: I don't think I cared all that much about watching that creature's flight, because even now in the middle of life, it is the tenderness of my aunt's touch that I can't forget. That touch told me I belonged. I mattered enough for her to help me notice something I wouldn't otherwise have seen. And in the process, her care invited mine.

A few minutes later we caught up with our family and did the things I suppose you do on summer vacations with relatives you don't see but once a year. Don't ask me what. Because though our bird-watching moment might have been forgettable to most, it's the only part about that trip I remember.

From that point on, I began to learn that living well and being fully alive meant stopping long enough to help another person see or feel or care. The only life that makes any sense is this one: the one of suffering *with* others. It's where we peek at a slice of an altogether otherworldly community, one that was and is and is to come.

Real life.

Somehow, those communities are connected. And somehow, that connection doesn't seem so small.

All of the places of our lives are sanctuaries; some of them just happen to have steeples. And all of the people in our lives are saints; it is just that some of them have day jobs and most will never have feast days named for them.

—Robert Benson, *Between the Dreaming and the Coming True*

It doesn't come naturally, this business of caring for others. Though I am quite certain that life at its fullest means bending over someone else, close enough to brush their skin with yours so that they see beyond the moment, it has never been an easy concept for me to pick up. The secret of compassion might be buried in textbooks or explained in seminars, but I have rarely learned it there.

Saints with day jobs, however, have taught me over and over. Even when I didn't know it at the time.

Every June, July, and August of my high school years, I was a proud member of the Callahan Real Estate girls' softball team of Wheat Ridge, Colorado. I'd been playing Little League on other teams since I was in second grade and loved everything about it: the sun on my face, the snacks after games, the laughs with my friends. There was nothing like standing around a park in the summer, tossing a ball back and forth or watching a batter connect to a pitch every now and then, until the game was over and you sat around the bleachers drinking Pepsi or Mountain Dew, watching the next game. It was my kind of sport.

By my teenage years, however, the watching had turned to serious competition, and most of my friends turned to other fun. I decided to keep playing. Our high school didn't yet offer sports like softball or soccer for girls (it was the early 1970s, after all, before Title 9 made an impact), so suburban recreational centers filled the gap during the summer months. They offered all kinds of leagues for all levels of play.

I told my parents I wanted to play for Callahan Real Estate. Joining this particular team, they reminded me, wouldn't be easy. The players were all older, mostly juniors and seniors, and I was only a sophomore. They'd been playing together for a few years. I was coming in from another team. And while they already knew all their positions, I had merely stood wherever the coach put me. I hadn't focused long enough to excel at any one spot.

I was ready to try. So my parents took a chance and sent me to the recreation center to register. I signed my name, handed them a check, and instantly belonged to the team. The team's winning record was better than all my Little League teams combined. I'd heard some girls at the center talk: Callahan had a pitcher whose windmill-style speed didn't give batters a chance, a shortstop who might as well have been a brick wall since nothing got by her, an outfielder who caught every pop fly, and a catcher with an arm that would peg any idiot who thought she could steal second base. Team members wore cool white cotton shirts with the gold-and-blue Callahan logo on the back, and matching baggy blue pants with a gold line down the side. They hit every time they were at the plate and caught every ball that cracked its way into the sky.

They were good. My old softball friends confirmed it when I called to tell them I'd joined Callahan. They warned me that Callahan's coach was really tough and mean and hard-nosed. Good luck.

I showed up for practice early and nervous. A few girls were already warming up, playing catch, or stretching. I joined them and waited. Soon a beat-up station wagon slowed into the parking lot. A tall but sturdy girl with short brown hair got out of the car, and a shorter, maternal version of the girl did too. Together they lugged over a duffel bag of bats and balls. The mom made another trip to the car for the bases and waddled out to the infield, bent over each white padded square, and shoved a steel peg into the ground to keep the bases from moving.

Her daughter came over to the dugout and introduced herself to me.

"My name's Jo," she said, pushing back the bangs from her eyes and smiling wide. "Jo Ridley. I'm the catcher."

"Cool—we have the same name." I relaxed. "I'm Jo too," I said.

She tossed me a ball to warm up. It only took a few throws to realize the rumors about her were true; my glove burned each time I caught the ball. A few other girls joined us by the dugout, talking and stretching and tossing softballs. Kathy, the pitcher, looked more glamorous than she did cutthroat; Leslie, the shortstop, was solid muscle but hardly a brick wall; and Debbie, the center fielder, seemed as easygoing as a California surfer. Kathy pulled her hair up in a ponytail. Leslie tied her cleats. Debbie cracked sunflower seeds. I caught Jo's burning throws and wondered when the coach would get here.

"What position do you play?" Jo asked, sailing a ripper into my palm.

I shrugged.

"We need a first baseman. Ours graduated last year," she said.

I liked that idea. I knew you didn't have to move much when you played first base, and I figured I could at least catch the throws of players like Jo or Leslie. My glove was thick and big; if I held it like a target for them, one foot on the bag, I could do it.

"Sounds good," I said, "if the coach thinks so."

They laughed as if I'd missed a joke until the joke stepped up to the plate and hollered. It was Jo's mom, the woman who'd just wrestled with the stakes in the infield. Pudgy. Short. Still in her house slippers. She wore wide denim shorts and a sleeveless flower-print blouse. A few curlers were pinned on top of her head. Her sunglasses were pointy.

"Come on, girls," she screeched. "Let's get this thing started."

Jo nodded over to the woman behind home plate and back at me with that same grin.

"That's the coach," she said, rolling a few balls in the direction of the backstop like she was bowling.

"Your mom's the coach?!" My hand was tingling.

"Yeah, the real coach quit two years ago. He said he had other things to do. And Callahan wouldn't sponsor us if we didn't get a coach." She grabbed a catcher's mask. "So my mom volunteered."

It was that simple. Then Jo jogged over to the oddity around home plate, and Kathy, Leslie, and the others followed. Somehow I felt my feet pick themselves up, and soon I was standing with the team in the circle, staring, listening, wondering about my friends at the mall.

"Okay, girls, new season. Same competition, give or take a few," Mrs. Ridley said. She sniffled, pulled a tissue from her pocket, blew her nose, and shoved the tissue back in the pocket. Then she looked at me. "My Jo tells me you're a Jo too. That's funny. But welcome!" She grinned like her daughter. "And you play first base. That's good for us because I think we need a first baseman, don't we, girls?" She looked at the team, who nodded collectively, and then she scratched her head, as if the curlers were itchy, before she turned back to me. "Well, Jo, I'll bet you'll do a great job at first base." Mrs. Ridley then picked up a bat and pounded home plate as though she were killing a rodent. "Geez, it's a scorcher, isn't it? Anyway, get a good drink of water and head on out to your positions, everyone!"

We guzzled before jogging to our spots. The sun hammered us, and I stood close to my base. Then the pudgy woman in curlers tossed a soft-ball above her head, grabbed the bat with both hands, and pulled it around with all her might so she could meet the ball on its way down. She hit a grounder to us, belting out orders about whom to throw it to. She did it again. And again. Most of the time, it worked. Sometimes the ball dropped with a thud on the plate. She'd pick it up and try again, hitting to Leslie, who'd devour the ball and fling it over to my target. I'd lob it back to Jo, who'd hand the ball to her mom again. Mrs. Ridley would toss it up and swing, this way or that, until someone else would field it and throw it to my glove.

After about forty-five minutes, she'd had enough. It *was* hot. She tossed the bat toward the fence, mopped her sweaty forehead with her tissue, and called for a water break. She asked Kathy to practice her pitches; we were moving into batting practice.

Mrs. Ridley then summoned outfielders one by one to the plate. She said if her players could hit off Kathy's windmill rocket, she thought they could hit off any pitcher. So she'd stand a few feet from home plate and clap her hands a lot to encourage us. She'd rattle off the same lines of instruction each time: *Elbow up. Watch the ball. Concentrate. Step into it. Follow through.*

Sometimes she'd move closer, turn the player's shoulders slightly to better position her for a hit, and return to her cheering and clapping. And her daughter—by now dressed from head to toe in catcher's gear—would repeat her mom's comments: *Elbow up. Watch the ball. Concentrate.*

"You can do it!" Mrs. Ridley would say each time, clapping and shaking and staring. Waiting. Hoping. And to my amazement, most did.

When every girl finally had batted—even I had managed a single—Mrs. Ridley called us in again around the plate. Her curlers loose, her flower-print blouse stained all around her armpits. Dust smudged her cheeks, which by now were bright red. Her belly jiggled. She told us we'd done a good job for the first practice and would meet again day after tomorrow. Same time and place. Right now she had to go back to work and asked if someone else would drive Jo home. Debbie nodded.

Before she left, Mrs. Ridley handed us schedules for the summer's games and tournaments and phone lists for the team. Then she took off her glasses.

"I'm expecting us to go all the way this year," she said, staring as seriously as she had during batting practice. Her eyes—brown and bare—moved gently across ours. *All the way* meant representing Colorado in a national tournament in Corpus Christi, Texas. In August. If we qualified, Callahan would pay our way.

"We just have to play hard, girls," she said, "and play together. Any questions?" Then she smiled before taking a curler off her head.

That was it? As I stood there in that June heat, even a rookie like me could tell this didn't sound like much of a strategy. Weren't we supposed to have drills and tactics and stuff? Wasn't this competitive league supposed to be a little more, well, serious?

I looked around at my teammates as Mrs. Ridley repeated herself. No one said anything. They didn't seem to mind what we were hearing. Maybe they figured this was better than nothing.

Maybe it was.

I watched Mrs. Ridley drive away and wondered if I'd made the right decision. Surely we'd be losers, and my old friends would all tease me on their way to the mall. I turned toward the parking lot, but Jo and Debbie and the others didn't let me sulk for long. They were going for a hamburger and a movie and I was welcome to come along.

After that first practice and the next, during each game and tournament throughout the summer, we did the only things Jo's mom ever told us to do: we played hard and we played together. Few opponents ever hit Kathy's pitches. And if they did, the ball never got past Leslie. I caught any throws she'd make, and Jo, well, she snagged more foul balls than anyone could remember. We won enough games so that we really did go all the way in August, compliments of Callahan Real Estate, to a state that was so hot and humid we collapsed after the first two games. But no matter.

We were friends. And that had happened because we were a team, a team where I belonged. Kept alive each time a pudgy middle-aged mom—who didn't seem to know a lot about softball except that her daughter loved it—stepped onto a hot dusty baseball field to help a bunch of high school girls work toward a dream.

To this day, I can still see Coach Ridley sweating or clapping or struggling to swing that bat and hit us grounders.

For centuries the church has confronted the human community with role models of greatness. We call them saints when what we really often mean to say is "icon," "star," "hero," ones so possessed by an internal vision of divine goodness that they give us a glimpse of the face of God in the center of the human. They give us a taste of the possibilities of greatness in ourselves.

—Joan Chittister, *A Passion for Life:*
Fragments of the Face of God

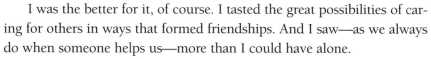

I was the better for it, of course. I tasted the great possibilities of caring for others in ways that formed friendships. And I saw—as we always do when someone helps us—more than I could have alone.

But it wasn't easy. Or fashionable. Or quick. That is not the nature of this type of passion. The word *compassion*, its history really, makes that clear. The Latin prefix *com*—which means "together"—gives us words we can't live without: *communication, communion, community.* The Latin infinitive *pati*, which in present tense is "suffer"—gives us a word I don't necessarily like: *patient*. From its past participle, *pass*, stems "the suffering of Christ on the cross." (*Patient* comes from the Latin *patiens*, from *patior,* "to suffer" or "to bear." The patient, in this case, is truly *passive*—enduring and tolerating *patiently* any necessary suffering.)

Reading such history is piercing in a way both good and bad: knowing that this word means to suffer (like Christ on the cross) *with* another person, or to enter *into* someone else's struggle with passive endurance, shoots straight through my restless independence. It hits grounders at my addiction to comfort. And yet I know, from intuition and experience, it is *com-passion* alone that redefines living, making it full and rich. Vigorous and sweaty.

Present and active. A living Word.

When I let this word's history dictate its future, one thing becomes clear: anyone qualifies. Anyone can be present. Active. Clapping like Mrs. Ridley. No expertise or specialty is required to struggle with another; I only have to see a need and step toward it.

We find compassion among all types of people in all kinds of places. We read about it in the news or watch it in the lives of those around us. Some friends—and no doubt you have a few like them—seem to be born caring for others. Compassion circulates in their veins and spills out of their every deed of every day. They patch up wounds, break down walls, or toss out softballs. They kiss scraped knees, fix dis-eased bodies, and empty urinals, because life doesn't make sense to them without such intersections. We call them *caregivers*.

I'm not one of them. Not naturally, at least. This holy gift was not dropped into my personality at birth like a song or a talent. Believe me (and my husband) when I say: I'm not wired this way. If someone doesn't tap me on my shoulder to point out the smallest of needs, my vision, and therefore, my world, stays very small. My instincts tend to focus mostly on the center of a cul-de-sac self that still doesn't easily move beyond my own driveway, beyond the familiar, the safe, the tidy.

But *none* of that is life-giving. Nor are any of the gizmos the marketing experts claim will make our lives better. I can't conjure up compassion or buy it online. No, if I'm ever to belong to this community of *sufferers-with*, I need nothing short of a transfusion. New blood. I need the ongoing miracle of Mercy made flesh, found first in the Man of Sorrows who entered mine, who struggled through human death to re-create my selfish life. So that even as the shadows of pain and the stench of death come around me, I can feel a hand on my shoulder and a quiet but holy whisper in my ear saying, "Look there."

> *If I did not believe, if I did not make what is called an act of faith (and each act of faith increases our faith, and our capacity for faith), if I did not have faith that the works of mercy do lighten the sum total of suffering in the world, so that those who are suffering on both sides of this ghastly struggle somehow mysteriously find their pain lifted and some balm of consolation poured on their wounds, if I did not believe these things, the problem of evil would indeed be overwhelming.*

—Dorothy Day, *On Pilgrimage*

They were strange years, the few after I graduated from high school softball games, then college classes, and entered the professional world of education. I'd moved to Denver, a city where jobs were scarce. But I'd been offered one at a suburban high school, teaching students at the bottom of the ladder and working with girls in a sport I knew little about.

The player became a coach.

I hadn't played much basketball, only a few seasons in my own high school and in college intramurals when friends needed an extra body to run up and down the court. I wasn't a strategist of the game or even a fan. But experience led me to believe I didn't need much to organize a practice or run a drill. I'd at least learned how to clap by then.

So in November of 1982, I walked into the gym and met fifteen players who would fill the roster of our junior varsity team, most of them sophomores and in their first year of high school. I tossed them some basketballs and told them to practice shooting. I watched. A few girls managed to connect with the basket, a few rebounded, and a few seemed to know how to dribble. This was a good start, I thought, before I saw Stephanie.

Taller than the other girls and more energetic than all of them put together, Stephanie's wide smile might have compensated for her lack of ability in junior high. Not now. She was lanky and raw, clumsy but determined. Her brother had told her she should try out for the team, and he would help her. Her mother had agreed and cheered her on as well. Her father, well, she didn't see him much. He didn't live with them and that was just fine with her. So here she was, bouncing around the court in her T-shirt and shorts, tripping on her teammates, ecstatic just to be on the team.

We ran drills to practice layups. Everyone knew what to do except Stephanie. I took extra time for her, but the other players didn't mind. She was tall, after all—a good four inches above the others. Her black ponytail standing straight off her head made her seem even taller. Her shoulders were broad and her skin darker than everyone else's. She looked as intimidating as a sophomore girl in high school could, even if she smiled too much and didn't know what she was doing. None of us did.

Every day after school I met Stephanie and her teammates on the court. We ran the same drills, practiced the same shots, and talked about the same goals until, finally, we played our first game. Stephanie beamed as she stepped onto that court in her brand-new blue polyester uniform. As if she'd never worn such a beautiful outfit. As if it made her a star.

We lost. But the next day, Stephanie came early to practice. She wanted to work on some things her brother had taught her. So I shrugged and clapped and watched as she'd pound the floor with the ball and chuck it toward the basket, where it'd ricochet off the backboard. She'd chase it down and try again. And again. Pounding and chucking and chasing. She threw so much energy and muscle into each movement, I began to worry that our most intimidating player might hurt herself.

But her teammates, her friends, walked in. She flashed that smile and joined them for layups. Sometimes the ball would go in the net, and sometimes it wouldn't. No matter. Stephanie would thump down the court and try again. She'd rebound and pass, trip, or chase. The girl was falling in love with the game.

For all the effort, though, and all the clapping, we did not score many points during the next several games. By mid-January, our team had turned in grand efforts but few wins, and we were slowly falling into last place in our league. We had one more month to turn things around. When I gathered the girls into a huddle during one practice to talk about playing hard and playing together, Stephanie nodded her head and patted her teammates on the back.

"We can do it, everybody! We can do it," she said, clapping. Hopeful. Focused. What mattered to her was that we played at all.

We won the next game.

One afternoon in early February, the head girls' basketball coach called me into his office. I was expecting to be chastised for our lousy record and so had prepared a pack of excuses I'd hoped would earn me another year's contract. Instead, he pointed toward a chair, asked me to sit down, and cleared his throat. He took the chair opposite me, his face serious. I swallowed.

"I just got a phone call," he said, looking away. He took a breath so that his shoulders lifted and fell. He glanced back at me. "It was the police. It's not good."

He explained that the father of one of our girls had taken a gun to his ex-wife, son, and daughter before turning it on himself. Neighbors had heard the shots, called the police, and all four bodies were found on the living room floor.

It was Stephanie. And her brother. And her mom.

I stared. At him. At nothing. At evil.

I couldn't imagine her any other way but full of energy and excitement. And I did not want to.

Now I had to. My head coach was asking me to tell Stephanie's teammates, and to decide how much, if any, of the season we wanted to finish. My eyes filled. My ears ached. But somehow I nodded, shuffled my feet, made my way to the gym where a group of fourteen high school girls were laughing and dribbling and warming up. I gathered them into a huddle, and I whispered the news.

Stephanie was gone.

But even amid the screams and agony, those girls could not, and would not, think of ending their season. They would play for their teammate from here on out. They would play together. For her.

I don't remember how I got there, but the next thing I knew I was in my apartment. I picked up the phone and dialed. My friend Joyce answered, as I hoped she would. She and her husband lived only a few miles from me, friends because of their involvement with Christian ministries. I'd moved to Denver in part to be near them, drawn to their lives, their faith, as models a few years older than I was.

I tried hard to explain to Joyce what had happened to Stephanie. But how do you say something like that? Why should you ever have to? So I mumbled something about a player . . . and I didn't quite know what to . . . I wasn't sure how to . . . what was the next . . .

"I'll be right over," she said softly. Directly. Instinctively.

I hung up the phone, I think. And soon Joyce knocked on my door. She hugged me. Then she sat on my couch. I cried some; so did she, and I talked a little. We ate pasta. She listened.

She stayed with me until I fell asleep.

I wish I could tell you that our junior varsity basketball team won the rest of that season in honor of their teammate. Or that Joyce offered more insights and pasta as comfort over the coming weeks. Or even that Stephanie's funeral was a sobering but soothing tribute that helped us all process the horror of her loss.

The truth is those details are a blur. What is clear is this: in a terrible afternoon during a bumpy, bruised year, we lost the vibrant spirit of a beautiful young girl. And for one profound evening, I experienced the compassion of a friend.

Neither is something you can forget.

"But please, please—won't you—can't you give me something that will cure Mother?" Up till then he had been looking at the Lion's great front feet and the huge claws on them; now, in his despair, he looked up at its face. What he saw surprised him as much as anything in his whole life. For the tawny face was bent down near his own and (wonder of wonders) great shining tears stood in the Lion's eyes. They were such big, bright tears compared with Digory's own that for a moment he felt as if the Lion must really be sorrier about his Mother than he was himself.

"My son, my son," said Aslan. "I know. Grief is great. Only you and I in
this land know that yet. Let us be good to one another."

—C. S. Lewis, *The Magician's Nephew,*

Book 1 in The Chronicles of Narnia

Some memories never leave us. Like a tradition at Christmas, the language and legends of *com-passion* linger long. They speak across cultures, bringing strangers to each other, and softening souls with otherworldly grace. Compassion, I have come to believe, is our greatest gift and our surest legacy, the most visible sign that we are not—and were not and will not be—alone. It is how we're meant to live.

Once, when I was driving through Virginia, I caught a stomach virus, turned sick and pale and weak. A friend of a friend let me stay in his family's home, so they could bring me soup and clean up after me.

Once, when I was working at a conference in Cambridge, England, friends I'd known only a week discovered it was my birthday. They threw a party for me on the bank of the Cam River and sang to me as I blew out candles on a scone.

More than once, in the Harlem neighborhood where my husband and I lived, neighbors knocked on our door with chocolate cakes or reminders to move our car on street-cleaning days (so we wouldn't be ticketed). They'd bring in our garbage cans for us on trash day, and show us that even in a city of eight million, in a community caricatured more for its crime than its compassion, real neighbors still existed.

I saw it again when writer-friends I hardly knew brought my husband and me dinner every night for two weeks while I recovered from hip surgery. Or when friends came to my mother's funeral, though they'd never met her. Or when the couple next door to us in this New England town where we now live insisted we come for dinner the day after we'd moved in.

Most recently I was completely transformed by compassion when I watched strangers in green scrubs wander in and out of the intensive care unit where my father's second wife lay struggling for her life. As I sat beside my dad, across from Nanci's brother and sister-in-law, I saw doctors, specialists, and nurses—whose work daily took them to death's intersection with life—care so deeply I wondered if this was their only passion. They used terms like *palliative care* and *quality of life*, which we all knew made death as painless as possible for the sick, though not necessarily for the well. And late one afternoon, when Mary Margaret walked in, introduced herself as the night-shift nurse, we saw it close up again. A youthful-looking woman with auburn hair, she wore bright pink scrubs with little Disney characters on them and caressed Nanci's hand so gently I thought maybe they were friends. She dabbed Nanci's forehead, fluffed her pillow carefully, and filled up the water pitcher for my dad. Then she went and stood beside him. She put her hand on his shoulder. And as she did, her eyes filled up.

We lost Nanci that night. Mary Margaret cried with us. And I realized that the quality of a person's life could never be determined by gadgets or tubes, surgeries or monitors. But rather by the hands that held a dying wife, a sister, a friend—the people around the bed of a woman in her final breaths of life. Here. Suffering with her. Together. Remembering.

Yes, there are some things we can't avoid, though God knows we want to. I do, at least. Yet, in the middle of such nightmares, we are comforted by the grace of a hand, the kindness of a stranger-turned-friend, the presence simply of another pain-bearer that helps us endure. Helps us live. Makes us want to do the same for others.

Sometimes, though, I just want life as we know it to go on. Loved ones to be safe. Friends to be well. Families to be together. Alive. Today. Present. Active.

Instead, each night is full of sorrow, each morning tight with hope. To live in this world, broken and sick as it is, I know, is to experience both. To live well, wholly human, fully alive, is to be pricked and broken by both the pain and the healing, the loneliness and the friendship, the tragedies and the gifts. It is to step in close to another, to touch a shoulder, and to receive a touch as well.

How else would we notice the birds? How else would we work toward the possibilities of a dream, survive the evils of the age, lose the love of a lifetime, if not for the tapping and pointing and presence of another?

Yes, indeed, let us be good to one another.

*A capacity for going overboard is a
requisite for a full-grown mind.*
—Dawn Powell

jump (jŭmp) [Perhaps Middle English
jumpen, *to jump* (sense uncertain)] verb.

To spring off the ground or other base by a
muscular effort of the legs and feet.

To take prompt advantage; respond quickly;
jump at a bargain.

To enter eagerly into an activity; plunge.

EPILOGUE

Jumping Overboard

Unbeing dead isn't being alive.
—e. e. cummings

The doorbell rang. My husband and I were expecting an old friend from the suburban Christian college where I once taught. He and his Latina wife had come to visit New York City, and we were taking them to lunch at the Muslim café a few blocks from our Harlem apartment. It had been many months since we last saw one another, and we were looking forward to our reunion.

We walked around the corner to the restaurant, a cozy place on the first floor of a building that housed the mosque where Malcolm X preached. Though we were usually the only pale-skinned customers in the place, this had become a favorite café since we moved into the neighborhood. The food and the service were always good.

Sitting at a table near the window, we sipped hot coffee and enjoyed the warm taste of friendship. We told old stories and new, talked of

EPILOGUE

writing and romance, faith and cultures, the past and the future, covering a hundred other topics the way old friends do.

I glanced up from our conversation and noticed a woman about my age sitting at the table beside us. She was eating alone, but she did not seem lonely; her smooth round face conveyed a soft familiarity that I could not help but admire. Her black hair was brushed neatly back, and her gentle brown eyes studied the other eyes and faces in the room.

Had I met her before? No, I did not think so.

Soon after our grits and chicken arrived, I looked again at the woman and saw her do something I had never seen before or since: each time we laughed, she did too. Each time our faces turned serious in our discussion, hers did too. If someone at our table made a strong point or told a funny story, she'd nod her head, purse her brow, or chuckle as if she knew exactly what we meant. This woman—this absolute stranger—was listening to every word and detail and paragraph of our entire conversation, actively and politely affirming everything we said as she finished her soup.

By the time our desserts arrived, the woman got up to leave. I wondered what she might be thinking, having listened so intently to our discussion. She went to the counter to pay her bill, gathered her coat and bags, and smiled at me as she walked out the door. I smiled back, thinking it odd but not altogether strange—this was New York, after all. The sheer density of the city often invited strangers into each other's lives.

I just hoped she enjoyed our time together.

We drank our last cup of coffee, and my husband asked the waiter for the check. He began arguing with our friends over the bill. We insisted it was our treat because they were visiting, but they seemed to think this was their idea. Before we could agree, the tall man who had served our meal interrupted us.

That is when he said the strangest thing I have heard in a restaurant anywhere: "You don't have a bill."

He picked up our plates and shuffled around us. When his words actually registered in our brains, all four of us turned to the waiter.

"Excuse me?" I stared blankly, matching the expressions of the others around our table. We asked if he was mistaken. He shook his head. We wondered if he was playing a joke on us. He did not smile.

"The woman sitting next to you?" He paused so we'd remember. "She wanted to buy your lunch. And she did."

We stared at the empty table beside us. It was the first time during our entire visit that we were silent.

With that, the waiter walked toward the kitchen. We looked at each other, still wondering if we'd heard right, wondering if we really were in New York City, wondering what in the world had just happened. Still quiet, heads shaking, we watched the waiter come back to our table from the kitchen. He handed me a small business card.

"Oh, she left you this."

I read the card aloud: "Thank you for a nice lunch. If you want to thank me, you can call me. Here's my phone number. God bless you— Desiree."

She *had* paid our bill. We walked back to our apartment, talking all the way about the fact that we had just been given a free lunch in New York City.

As if repeating the story would help us believe. (It did, of course.)

I called Desiree, and I stumbled over my words. Why would she have been so kind, so gracious, to four strangers? Why did she go out of her way to do something so unexpected and so out of the ordinary? I rambled, looking for some rational thought to hold on to, still unsure how to make sense of this.

"I'm a Christian too," she told me. Usually she liked to go to that café for breakfast, but she said yesterday for some reason she had decided to stop there for lunch on her way to work. She told me she was a part-time clerk at the post office. And she just enjoyed us. That's all.

"It was nice listening to a lively conversation from brothers and sisters in the Lord," she said softly. It was no big deal, she said, adding that perhaps sometime we'd run into each other again.

Perhaps we would.

I hung up the phone stunned and humbled by Desiree's act of charity. I still am every time I remember it.

But if I have learned anything about the generosity of passion across the years and pages and adventures, it is this: like the wonder of waves on a beach, it surprises me each time I encounter it (or it encounters me). And it is equally delightful and attractive each time it drops onto the shore where I happen to be standing. That doesn't change.

Why else would I look for the next wave as it comes to splash me?

This is what I have seen to be good: it is fitting to eat and drink and find enjoyment in all the toil with which one toils under the sun the few days of the life God gives us; for this is our lot. Likewise all to whom God gives wealth and possessions and whom he enables to enjoy them, and to accept their lot and find enjoyment in their toil—this is the gift of God. For they will scarcely brood over the days of their lives, because God keeps them occupied with the joy of their hearts.

—Ecclesiastes 5:18-20, NRSV

I started with a dream. I was drowning and wasn't even fighting for a breath. The sheer terror of such indifference woke me, and in a most surprising way, nudged me overboard. It brought me here, to this ecclesiastical land marked with wonder and wanderlust, agony and irony, love and loveliness—*gladness of heart*—where I am realizing it *is* good and proper to drink in every last drop God gives.

This is our lot. God's is to rescue drowning souls. Again and again.

Which is a good thing since, as you know by now, I need saving many times over. I wander. I forget. I fail or I ignore. And even when I remember, I want this life, this faith, this passion really, to be a smooth, silky lake. Not one with storms or whirlwinds. Please give me living I can fit into my pocket or a formula I can pass on to others. As if anyone whose arms are flailing and whose head is almost under could be rescued by ten steps or five principles or seven habits.

No, this word *passion* is messy. This suffering of God's Son, these beautiful acts of heroism or romance, these objects of devotion or desires, all a mess. These seven letters move, change, and disguise themselves a hundred times over. Even in the muddle, though, even in the chaos of our culture and streets, somehow passion groans and sings, sometimes even chuckles, if we'll listen. It rides through excruciating affliction to glorious wonder, from tragic pain to transformed beauty, from dying and decay to living and redemption. In other words—and forgive me for being crass here—the ship's already going down. So we might as well jump.

Yes, indeed, why not fling ourselves overboard into this breathing, aching question *What does it mean to be alive?* Why not fling our beings into this word *passion*? It grows because we do; it keeps us from terrifying categories like "the walking dead"; it wraps itself around us like a life preserver wherever we are in the sea, tossed by waves.

And so each hand the Savior offers, each painting, each song or kiss or trial, each Communion Table or lunch bought by a stranger-turned-friend, brings us out of the darkness of our souls and into the light of *this* passion. Where we can see again the hope of heaven. Flogged on the back of a man, stretched out on the wood of a cross. For me, for you.

But wait a holy minute. Because when I go looking, I can't find him in the tomb. No crooked graveyard marker at all for him. How could that be? His organs failed, his lungs collapsed, his heart ripped apart and stopped entirely—witnessed by dozens of credible sources. And yet a few days later, he strolled on beaches and dusty roads. He walked into rooms and gardens. Breathing. Human. Living again. Irrational blood and bones. Defiant flesh and wounds. The mystery of the ages discovered in a holiday we call Easter, the connection to and foundation for all our other passions.

He became the only walking, laughing, cooking Dead Alive Man ever in history. Others witnessed that too.

Why did he do that?

To pay for our lunch. To become our sustenance. To enjoy us so we could enjoy others.

This passion surprises me always. It invites me—and you—from the here and now to the everlasting. Its home is a city where all types of souls gather around a table, listening to one another as friends, a place the apostle John calls a "Holy City, the new Jerusalem, coming down out of heaven from God, prepared as a bride beautifully dressed for her husband" (Revelation 21:2). The splendor of its streets and gates, walls, and rivers we can only imagine with each trip we take on this planet. The images and colors and shapes we can only hope for with each work of art we see here.

When we smell lilacs in full bloom, we can wonder if their scent comes from *that* tree of life. When we hear a Sunday organ, neighbors singing, we can wonder if it is a prelude of sounds to come. When we watch a child playing and skipping on the beach, we cannot help but think it is a portion of the gladness God will occupy us with forever.

All of which started this morning.

Life Preservers

Well, when one's lost, I suppose it's good advice to stay where you are until someone finds you. But who'd ever think to look for me here?
—Alice, in the film *Alice in Wonderland*

The following resources have served as life preservers for me. They've been tossed out to me at various stages and seasons in life when I needed words or music, images or sounds, to hang on to. They've offered direction and hope and a whole lot of glad tidings, helping me think about and feel the various meanings of passion, about what it means to stay alive even when alien pods are threatening on the horizon.

I'm grateful for each and toss them out to you as well, hoping you'll grab on to a few to help keep you afloat.

ART
Bastien-Lepage, Jules. *Joan of Arc* (oil on canvas) 1879.
Caravaggio, Michelangelo Merisi da. *The Incredulity of Saint Thomas* (oil on canvas) 1601–1602.

BOOKS

Baum, L. Frank. *The Wonderful Wizard of Oz*. New York: Sterling Publishing Co., 2005. First published 1900, children's fiction.

Benson, Robert. *Between the Dreaming and the Coming True: The Road Home to God*. San Francisco: HarperSanFrancisco, 1996. Memoir.

Buechner, Frederick. *Telling the Truth: The Gospel as Tragedy, Comedy, and Fairy Tale*. San Francisco: HarperSanFrancisco, 1977 (sermons).

——————. *Wishful Thinking: A Seeker's ABC*. Rev. ed. San Francisco: HarperSanFrancisco, 1993 (memoir).

Brooks, Geraldine. *Year of Wonders: A Novel of the Plague*. New York: Penguin, 2001.

Carroll, Lewis. *Alice's Adventures in Wonderland*. New York: Aladdin Classics/Simon and Schuster Children's Publishing Division, 2000 (first published 1865).

Day, Dorothy. *On Pilgrimage*. Grand Rapids, MI: William B. Eerdmans Publishing Company, 1999 (nonfiction, first published 1948).

Didion, Joan. *The Year of Magical Thinking*. New York: Knopf Publishing, 2005 (memoir) .

Dillard, Annie. *The Writing Life*. New York: Harper and Row, Publishers, 1989 (nonfiction).

Dubay, Thomas. *The Evidential Power of Beauty: Science and Theology Meet*. San Francisco: Ignatius Press, 1999.

Finney, Jack. *Invasion of the Body Snatchers*. New York: Simon and Schuster, 1998 (science fiction, originally published in 1954).

Frankl, Viktor E. *Man's Search for Meaning*. Trans. Ilse Lasch. Boston: Beacon Press, 2006 (memoir, originally published in 1946).

Guroian, Vigen. *Tending the Heart of Virtue: How Classic Stories Awaken a Child's Moral Imagination*. New York: Oxford University Press, 1998.

Krakauer, Jon. *Into the Wild*. New York: Anchor Books, 1997 (nonfiction).

Lewis, C. S. *The Magician's Nephew*. London: Bodley Head, 1955 (Book 1 in The Chronicles of Narnia; children's fantasy).

Lloyd-Jones, Sally. *The Jesus Storybook Bible: Every Story Whispers His Name*. Grand Rapids, MI: Zondervan 2007 (children's Bible).

Milne, A. A. *Winnie-the-Pooh*. Jacksonville, IL: Perma-Bound Books, 1926 (children's fiction).

Morgan, Robert J. *Then Sings My Soul: 150 of the World's Greatest Hymn Stories*. Nashville, TN: Thomas Nelson, 2003.

Muggeridge, Malcolm. *A Third Testament: A Modern Pilgrim Explores the Spiritual Wanderings of Augustine, Blake, Pascal, Tolstoy, Bonhoeffer, Kierkegaard, and Dostoevsky*. New York: Little, Brown and Company, 1976 (biography and autobiography).

Nicholson, William. *Shadowlands*. New York: Plume/Penguin Books, 1991 (drama).

Nouwen, Henri M., Don McNeill, and Douglas A. Morrison. *Compassion: A Reflection on the Christian Life*. New York: Doubleday, 1966.

Peterson, Eugene H. *The Message: The Bible in Contemporary Language* Colorado Springs, CO: NavPress Publishing Group, 2002.

—————————. *Subversive Spirituality*. Grand Rapids, MI: William B. Eerdmans Publishing Company, 1997.

Potok, Chaim. *My Name Is Asher Lev*. New York: Anchor Books, 2003 (fiction).

O'Connor, Flannery. *The Habit of Being*. Edited by Sally Fitzgerald. New York: Farrar, Straus and giroux, 1988 (letters).

—————————. *Mystery and Manners*. Edited by Sally and Robert Fitzgerald. New York: Farrar, Straus and Giroux, 1969 (essays).

Sayers, Dorothy L. "Towards a Christian Aesthetic" (essay) from *Letters to a Diminished Church: Passionate Arguments for the Relevance of Christian Doctrine*. Nashville, TN: Thomas Nelson, 2004.

——————.*The Man Born to Be King.* Grand Rapids, MI: William B. Eerdmans Publishing Company, 1970 (BBC radio play, first published 1941–1942).

Wangerin, Walter, Jr. *The Book of the Dun Cow.* New York: HarperCollins Publishers, 1978 (children's fantasy).

——————. *Ragman and Other Cries of Faith.* New York: Harper Collins Publishers, 1984 (nonfiction).

White, E. B. *Charlotte's Web.* New York: Harpercollins Publishers, 1952 (children's fiction).

Williams, Tennessee. *The Glass Menagerie.* New York: New Directions Books, 1999 (drama, first published 1945).

Wood, Ralph C. "Shadowlands—A Movie Review," *The Christian Century* 111, no. 6 (Feb. 23, 1994):200-02.

Wright, Vinita Hampton. *The Soul Tells a Story: Engaging Creativity with Spirituality in the Writing Life.* Downers Grove, IL: InterVarsity Press, 2005.

FILMS

Babette's Feast. Directed by Gabriel Axel. Panorama Film A/S, 1988, DVD (Danish film based on Isak Dinesen's short story of the same title).

It's a Wonderful Life. Directed by Frank Capra. Liberty Films, 1946.

The Gleaners and I. Directed by Agnes Varda. Ciné Tamaris, 2000 (French documentary film).

Strictly Ballroom. Directed by Baz Luhrmann. M & A Film Corporation, 1992.

MUSIC

Arends, Carolyn. *Seize the Day and Other Stories*. CD. Reunion Records ℗ and © Provident Label Group, 2000.

Carpenter, Mary Chapin. *Stones in the Road*. CD. Columbia/Nashville 1996 ℗ and © 1994 Sony BMG Music entertainment.

Jones, Norah. *Feels Like Home*. CD. Blue Note®/Capital Records, Inc. ℗ and © 2004 Capitol Records, Inc.

Lee, Peggy. *Miss Peggy Lee*. CD. Capitol. © 1998 Capitol Records, Inc.

Note on Word Definitions

Primary source for word pronunciation, etymology, and definition at chapter openings is *The American Heritage Dictionary of the English Language*, Fourth Edition (copyright © 2006 by Houghton Mifflin Company) with the following exceptions and supplemental sources:

- *art*: additional definition from Wordnet®3.0, Princeton University. http://dictionary.reference.com/browse/art/

- *suffer*: definitions from *Webster's Revised Unabridged Dictionary* (http://dictionary.reference.com/browse/suffer/) and http://www.answers.com/topic/suffering/

- *compassion*: author's definitions plus a definition from WordNet®3.0, Princeton University. http://dictionary.reference.com/browse/compassion/

How do you tell the story of your life—
of how you were born,
and the world you were born into,
and the world that was born in you?
—Frederick Buechner,
The Sacred Journey

About the Author

JO KADLECEK and her husband, Chris Gilbert—an Australian video guy—live on Boston's north shore in Beverly, Massachusetts. In 2006, Jo joined the faculty at Gordon College in Wenham, Massachusetts, where she teaches nonfiction writing, journalism, and communications courses. Most recently she also became senior communication writer for Gordon's Office of College Communication. Jo also teaches at church retreats and conferences across the country and continues to write for various publications. Visit the website for Jo and Chris: www.lamppostmedia.net/

More
FRESH AIR BOOKS®

Compassion:
Thoughts on Cultivating a Good Heart
Enhance your capacity to care by cultivating a compassionate heart. Chances are, someone you know could use a little of your time, a bit of your spirit. In this little book, several writers talk about how to adopt compassion as a way of life.
96 pages.

ISBN 978-0-8358-9955-0
$12.00

Forgiveness: Perspectives on Making Peace with Your Past
Go beyond forgiving and forgetting. Learn how to make peace with your past. The writers in this collection say forgiving does not require you to pretend you were never hurt. It does mean finding out how to heal the past in order to embrace the future.
96 pages

ISBN 978-0-8358-9956-7
$12.00

Talk That Matters:
30 Days to Better Relationships
Your relationships can improve
significantly when you know how to
speak with and listen to people better!
Discover ways to make meaningful
conversation possible. Short, practical
"lessons" lead you to real change.
160 pages

ISBN 978-1-935205-03-6
$15.95

The Chocolated-Covered Umbrella:
Discovering Your Dreamcode
Psychotherapist Tilda Norberg explains a
simple, holistic, and enjoyable way to let
dreams speak to you. The process is not
intended as therapy but as a way to explore
what your dreams are telling you. You can
open yourself to the Holy One in a new way
that leads to spiritual discovery.
160 pages

ISBN 978-1-935205-02-9
$14.95

Available from your local bookstore
online at www.freshairbooks.com
or by phone
1-800-972-0433